# Con





**Warning**

Much of this material will need to be prepared (photocopied and cut up) before lessons.

# Introduction

## What's in *Learning global lessons*?

*Learning global lessons* provides teacher's instructions and resources for 50 non-fiction literacy hours. It is divided into five units, each generating two weeks' work. Each unit focuses on a National Literacy Strategy genre, a Key Stage Two year and term, a graphic and a specific area of the world.

This innovative resource pack introduces a range of text types and draws on ActionAid's internationally recognised approach to literacy, Reflect. Resources and graphics from around the world support text, sentence and word level work suitable for years four, five and six.

*Learning global lessons* encourages pupils to consider all forms of text and their uses, eg lettering, numbers, symbols, signs, diagrams and graphics. It aims to develop pupils' literacy skills using relevant materials set in meaningful contexts.

A Reflect graphic: 24-hour recall circle

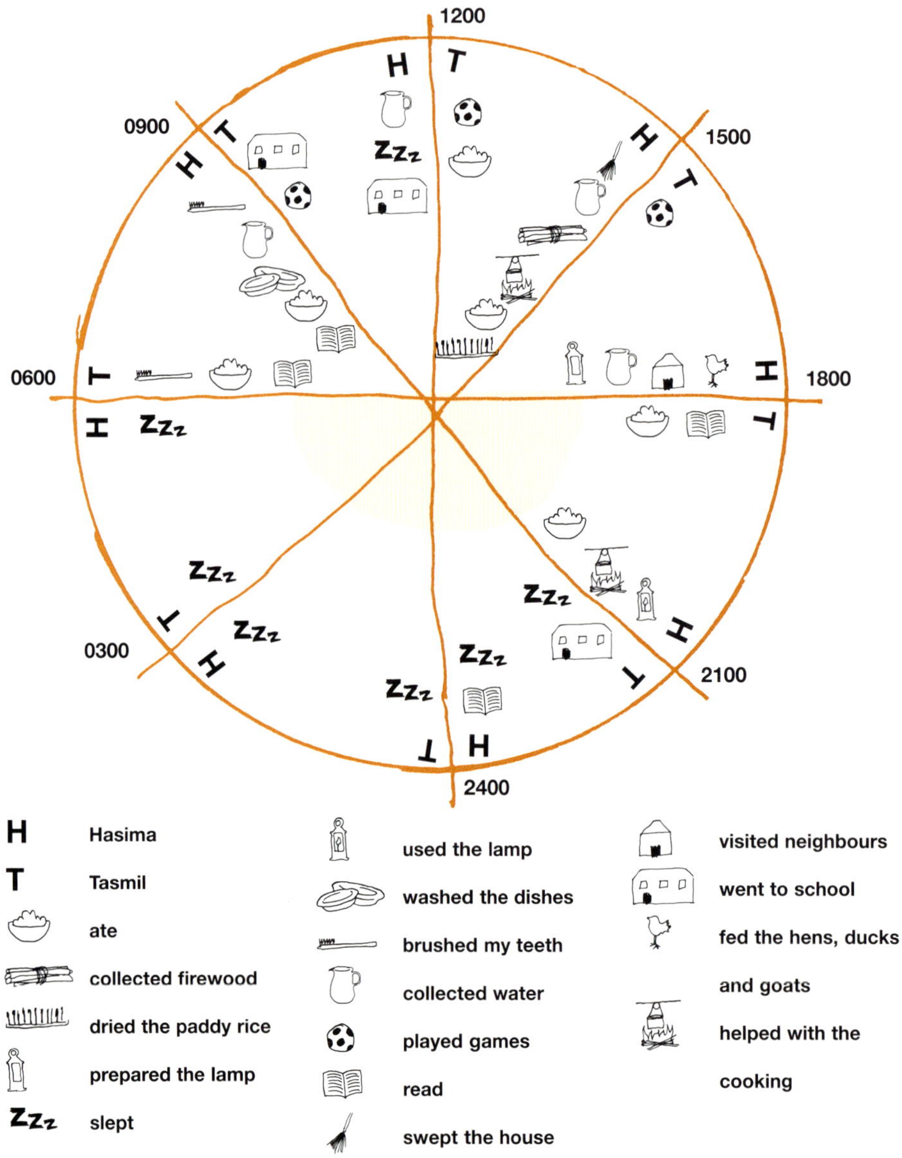


This 24-hour recall circle is used as a text to compare the jobs done by Tasmil (a boy) and Hasima (a girl) from Netrakona District, Bangladesh.

# The Reflect approach

In 1993 ActionAid introduced its innovative international literacy programme, Reflect. The Reflect approach is two to three times more successful than conventional approaches to teaching reading and writing and has been taken up by 40 countries around the world, through 200 different organisations.

- Reflect is open to adults and children. Learning takes place in a circle. To ensure learning is relevant to people's lives, the first session includes a discussion of local issues, which become the basis of units introduced later in the programme.

**"Previously we were not interested in education for our brothers and sisters, but now we encourage them to go to school because we feel that without education no one can claim oneself as a complete human being."**
**Hasina Begum**, a Reflect participant in Dhaka, Bangladesh

- Text books are not used in Reflect circles. Instead, learners draw graphics such as maps, calendars or matrices on the ground to depict a particular aspect of their lives. Constructed using local materials such as sticks, stones or leaves, typical graphics include maps showing natural resources or matrices showing the food people eat.
- The graphic is then transferred to a large sheet of paper using simple pictures. Key words are introduced as labels to match the pictures. These words are broken down into syllables and learned through participative class exercises.
- After each unit is completed, participants consider what they have learnt and decide on an action point which they can undertake to achieve change in their everyday lives.

PHOTO: JENNY MATTHEWS

**A Reflect circle in Mubende, Uganda.**



The Reflect approach can be applied to a range of situations. Groups from the developing world, UK, Ireland, Eastern Europe, Canada and the US have adapted the approach for adult literacy, community education, refugee education and teaching English. *Learning global lessons* demonstrates the many opportunities for a Reflect type approach within the National Literacy Strategy.

# Activity sheet • The story of Yakshi

Yakshi is a small organisation based in south-east India. In 1995 Yakshi used ActionAid's Reflect approach to reading and writing with a local community.

When the Reflect programme started, the community said they were very worried. This was because people were no longer attending an important meeting where local problems were talked about, called the *Gotti*.

After a while the community decided to set up the *Gotti* again in order to discuss local problems and learn to read and write. They made two maps of the local area. These showed how the area had changed over the past 30 years. Then they made a crop matrix, which showed the advantages and disadvantages of growing over 20 crops.

The community discussed the results for many weeks. They looked at the problems and made action points to improve the situation. One problem was people grew a lot of tobacco and cotton to sell to foreign countries and the price of these suddenly went down. This was because big companies sold them at cheaper prices. The second problem was tobacco and fertilisers were causing health problems for the community. The third problem was not enough water for the crops to grow.

The community agreed on several action points. They decided to grow a variety of food crops including cotton, rice, okra and peppers. This would mean they could eat healthy food and not rely totally on big companies.

Some people decided to grow crops without using fertilisers and everybody made a plan to repair old water tanks and clean the weeds away from the ponds in order to have more water for the crops.

When the discussions finished the people learnt to read and write the important words and sentences connected with the problems and action points. Recently the communities have written down over 250 songs from the area, a history of many families and villages and traditional stories, sayings and dances.

Today the *Gotti* is a vibrant meeting and offers real hope for the future. One member says that the *Gotti* "is a space to sit and talk, to share our happiness and sorrows and an opportunity to reflect".

# Reflect and the literacy hour

## The five non-fiction text types

### Instructions

**Purpose**

- to tell someone how to do or make something.

**Main features**

- statement of what is to be achieved;
- materials/equipment needed;
- sequenced steps to achieve the goal;
- temporal connectives;
- usually written in the present tense.

### Non-chronological report

**Purpose**

- to describe the way things are.

**Main features**

- general statement;
- facts about the topic;
- formal writing style;
- paragraphs, subheadings and illustrations;
- non-chronological;
- usually written in the present tense.

### Persuasion

**Purpose**

- to take a position on an issue and justify it.

**Main features**

- statement of the issue;
- arguments and justifications;
- summary;
- language associated with reasoning;
- emotive vocabulary;
- usually written in the present tense.

### Recount

**Purpose**

- to retell events.

**Main features**

- opening paragraph setting the scene;
- recount of events in chronological order;
- closing statement;
- temporal connectives;
- often written in the first or third person;
- usually written in the past tense.

### Explanation

**Purpose**

- to give an account of how or why something happens.

**Main features**

- general statement;
- sequenced explanation;
- action verbs;
- temporal and causal connectives;
- usually written in the present tense.



## Exchanging genres

The National Literacy Strategy includes a wide range of non-fiction text types or genres. Classifying texts according to genres is not always simple as overlap between genres often occurs. Genre exchange is present in several of the units, where pupils study one type of genre and produce another. Pupils are shown how to mix genres and create new ones for different audiences and purposes.

# The two-week plan

Every unit begins with a two-week plan. Each plan provides teacher's notes for ten literacy hours spanning two weeks. Each literacy hour is structured around the National Literacy Strategy guidelines.

## National Literacy Strategy guidelines: The literacy hour

Timings are approximate, eg it is feasible to combine the last two sections.

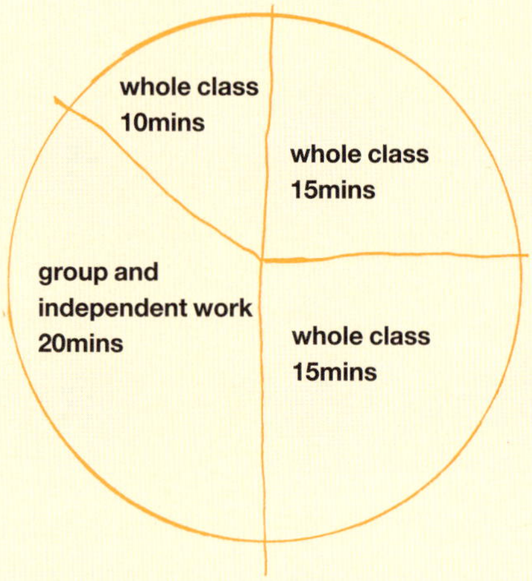


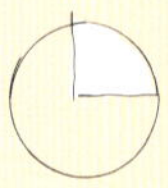

**Shared text work**
The teacher shares a text with the class and focuses on its purpose as a whole.

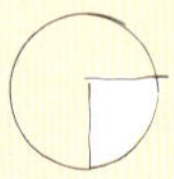

**Shared word and sentence work**
The teacher models how to read or write a text and focuses on word and sentence work.

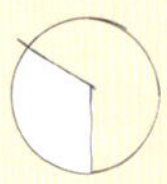

**Group and independent word and sentence work**
Pupils perform the above task.

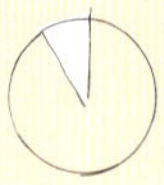

**Plenary**
Reviewing, reflecting and consolidating the main teaching points and presenting work covered in the lesson.

The progression of themes and skills is central to the two-week plan. These are developed and consolidated over the two weeks in order for pupils to produce a challenging piece of writing at the end of the unit.

Each week has a different but linked focus:

### Week one

**Focuses on understanding how and why a Reflect graphic is used.**

eg Unit four uses recount to look at a 24-hour recall circle in Netrakona District, Bangladesh. It highlights unequal gender workloads and action points to improve the situation.

### Week two

**Focuses on an issue relating to pupils' lives.**

eg Unit four uses recount to look at the unequal use of space in the school playground between girls and boys. Pupils create a graphic and consider ways of improving the situation.

## A balanced approach

The pack includes a range of learning and teaching activities. Examples of direct learning and teaching methods include teachers discussing text with individuals and groups and scaffolding pupils' understanding through the modelling of activities. Participative activities aim to heighten pupils' motivation and involvement, promote confidence, originality and sensitivity and make knowledge more explicit and personal.

The activities help pupils write clearly and concisely, so they can organise their thoughts and communicate with others in a way that is not open to misinterpretation. Discussing, framing, re-framing, selecting, presenting and explaining ideas help pupils to remember and understand.

## Stepping activities

Each unit includes stepped texts. Step 1 is the easiest step and step 4 provides a real challenge. The aim is for all pupils, regardless of ability, to start with step 1 and work through to step 4. As skills are acquired, the steps become unnecessary and pupils become more independent and confident writers.

**Example**

Underline nouns, action verbs and words to do with time in different ways.

step 4

Soon after, I travelled almost a kilometre to school on foot.

**Pupils are challenged further to demonstrate skills and understanding.**

step 3

Then I travelled to school on foot.

**Pupils consolidate skills and understanding.**

step 2

Then I travelled to school.

**Pupils develop skills and understanding.**

step 1

Then I walked to school.

**Pupils perform the task on the easiest text to ensure understanding.**

## Links with other subject areas

Reading and writing non-fiction is an important tool for learning across the curriculum. More will be learnt if other subjects are treated as vehicles for literacy work and tied to the literacy hour as much as possible.

Various sections of the pack relate directly to geography, art and science and afternoon follow-up suggestions are included in each unit.

## Learning global lessons and citizenship education

The pack also illustrates the role the literacy hour can play in citizenship education. The activities in *Learning global lessons:*

- encourage pupils to know about and understand the world and how they fit into it;
- investigate the links between pupils' lives and those of people in other parts of the world;
- counter negative images and stereotypes and give pupils an accurate representation of a place;
- provide pupils with opportunities to question and explore issues that are relevant to them now and in the future;
- evaluate pupils' own values and attitudes in the light of others;
- highlight reciprocal relationships between rights and responsibilities;
- help pupils understand the concept of social justice and enable them to take action to improve their world.



## The global citizenship ladder

Providing opportunities for pupils to learn through decision-making, participation and taking action can make a real contribution to the life of the class, school and community. In addition, issues covered such as bullying, recycling, food and the games girls and boys play are personal and relevant to pupils' daily lives.

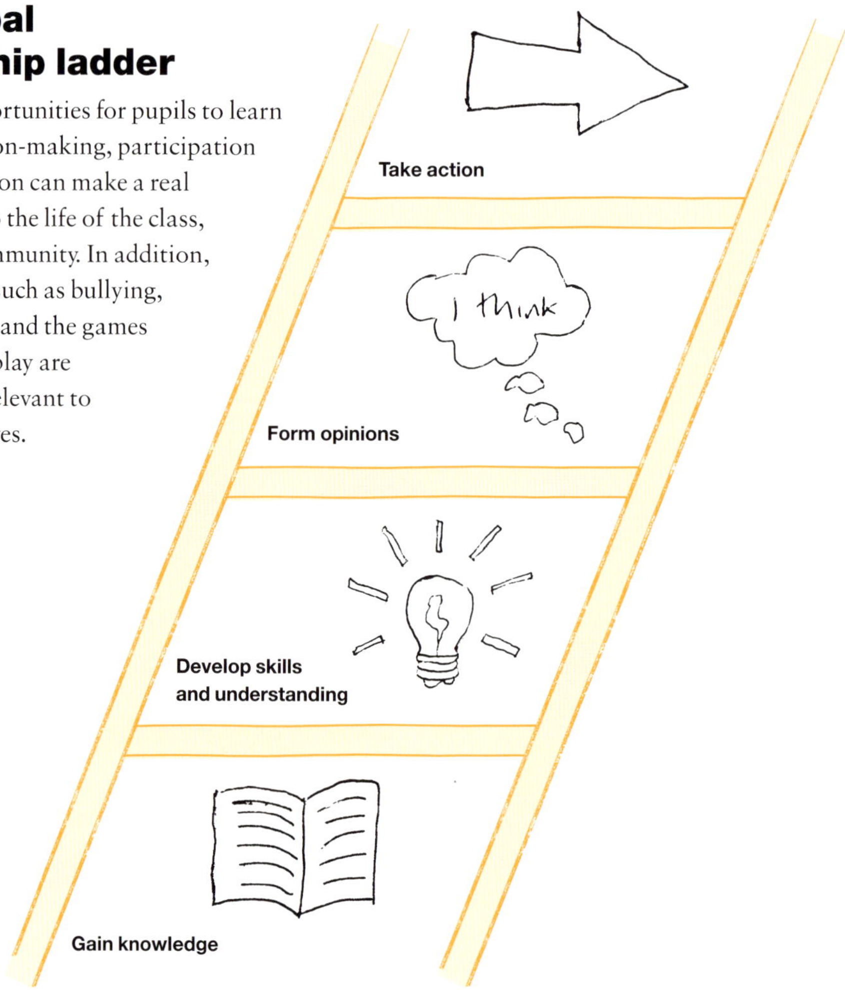

# Information about Uganda for teachers

Units 1 and 2 are based on information from Mubende District in Uganda. Uganda is an East African country lying on the equator. It is a landlocked country, but contains within its borders about half of Lake Victoria, the largest lake in Africa, about half of Lake Albert, and the whole of the smaller Lake Kioga. The total land area is 197,000km$^2$ with a further 44,000km$^2$ of inland water.

## Religion

Nearly half the population are Christian, one third follow traditional religions and there is a Muslim minority of around six per cent.

## Languages

Swahili (official language) and Luganda (local language) are widely spoken and numerous local languages are also spoken.

## Landscape and climate

Most of Uganda is a large plateau lying 1,000–1,400m above sea level, which stretches out between the highlands in the east, the Ruwenzori Mountains in the west and Lake Victoria in the south. Lakes Victoria, Kioga and Albert form part of the source region of the River Nile.



Most areas have two rainy seasons and receive an average 1,000–1,500mm rainfall a year. Temperatures range from 15°C–25°C, although these often drop in the hillier south-west. In the south, regions which have not been cleared for farming are thickly forested.

### Comparing Uganda with the UK

| | Uganda | UK |
|---|---|---|
| **Currency** | | |
| NUSh (New Ugandan Shillings) | 1,874NUSh (1999) | £1 |
| Per capita GDP (1996) | £188 | £12,250 |
| **Health and sanitation** | | |
| Life expectancy (1997) | 41 years | 77 years |
| Under-five mortality (deaths per 1,000 live births) (1997) | 109 | 7 |
| % of pop with access to safe water (1990–1997) | 46 | 100 |
| % of pop with access to adequate sanitation (1990–1997) | 57 | 100 |
| **Education** | | |
| % of primary school entrants reaching year five (1990–1995) | 55 | over 95 |
| % adults literate (1995) | 74 (male)<br>50 (female) | over 95 |
| No. of TV sets per 1,000 population (1995) | 13 | 448 |

## Mubende

Mubende is an area of forested plains and rolling hills in the centre of Uganda, 144km west of the capital city, Kampala. The total area of Mubende is 6,196km$^2$, of which 334km$^2$ is covered by surface water and shallow swampy valleys.

The area has two rainy seasons: March to May and September to November, with annual rainfall of 1,218mm, mostly concentrated in the north. Temperatures are high, ranging from 15°C–30°C throughout the year. In the past Mubende has experienced prolonged droughts, resulting in the drying up of rivers.

The population of Mubende is over 500,000, the majority of whom live in the rural areas as subsistence farmers. Most farmers produce food crops such as maize, beans, sweet potatoes, groundnuts, yams, pineapples and bananas. Cash crops are grown on larger farms and include coffee, cotton and tea. Food shortages are common when the rains are late.

ActionAid's Mubende programme focuses on empowering local communities to manage their own development. Every village selects representatives who then prioritise the needs of the village and supervise suitable development projects such as agricultural training, road building or water provision.

**"In the future I hope we can make progress without ActionAid. When ActionAid leaves, people will have skills, knowledge and capital, so they can continue to develop."**
**Dez Katangera**, chairman of a development committee

Less than half the adults in Mubende are literate (45 per cent) and this figure is as low as 35 per cent for women. As they have no experience of education, many adults place a low value on sending their children to school.

Although educating adults is the key to many aspects of development, adult literacy has been a very neglected area in Mubende. On a day-to-day basis, literacy means being able to read prices at the market, understand official documents, or simply the pleasure of reading a child's letter. In the long term, the whole community can benefit from the value parents place on education, particularly women.

**The landscape of Mubende.**

PHOTO: JENNY MATTHEWS

In 1997 ActionAid introduced its pioneering Reflect programme in Mubende. In its first year, 22 Reflect centres were constructed for 660 students. ActionAid also provides funding, training and equipment to raise standards in state primary schools, as well as setting up out-of-school centres where children can attend classes at flexible times to fit in with housework and farming.

When asked the difference he had noticed in his grandchildren since they attended an education centre, Desderio Salongo Walisimbi replied: "I have seen them read and write their names. I test them whenever I get the time and every other day I am amazed at the grasp they have on the knowledge they get from the centre."

# Information about Bangladesh for teachers

Units 3, 4 and 5 are based on information from Bangladesh. Units 3 and 5 look at Kukri Mukri Island in the south of Bangladesh and Unit 4 looks at Netrakona District in the north of the country.

Bangladesh is located in the northern corner of the Bay of Bengal and is crossed by the Tropic of Cancer. It has a land area of 147,960km$^2$, which is less than half the size of Britain. Bangladesh's population, however, is 127 million, which is more than twice that of Britain. Most of the people live in the countryside, but urban areas are growing rapidly. The land is fertile, because of the silt deposited by two large rivers, the Ganges and the Brahmaputra, but prone to cyclones and flooding.

## Religion

The vast majority of Bangladeshis follow Islam. Under 10 per cent of the population are Hindus. There are also small Buddhist and Christian minorities.

## Language

The official language of Bangladesh is Bengali.

## Landscape and climate



Bangladesh is located in the Ganges river delta, where the Ganges, Brahmaputra and Meghna rivers meet. Bangladesh lies on a fertile, alluvial plain where rice, tea and jute are grown. There are vast rainforests and swamps, and hills in the Sylhet region in the north-east and the Chittagong region in the south-east. Bangladesh has a tropical monsoon climate. Average annual rainfall is between 1,429–4,338mm, making Bangladesh one of the world's wettest countries.

### Comparing Bangladesh with the UK

| | **Bangladesh** | **UK** |
|---|---|---|
| **Currency** | | |
| Taka | 71 Taka (1998) | £1 |
| Per capita GDP (1996) | £162 | £12,250 |
| **Health and sanitation** | | |
| Life expectancy (1997) | 58 years | 77 years |
| Under-five mortality (deaths per 1,000 live births) (1997) | 137 | 7 |
| % of pop with access to safe water (1990–1997) | 95 | 100 |
| % of pop with access to adequate sanitation (1990–1997) | 43 | 100 |
| **Education** | | |
| % of primary school entrants reaching year five (1990–1995) | 47 | over 95 |
| % adults literate (1995) | 49 (male)<br>26 (female) | over 95 |
| No. of TV sets per 1,000 population (1995) | 6 | 448 |

## Netrakona

Netrakona is situated in the north-eastern corner of Bangladesh at the foot of the Garo Hills, once a region famous for producing rice and fish. Today, however, Netrakona is one of the poorest regions of Bangladesh and its low-lying terrain suffers frequently from flooding.

The roads in Netrakona are made of brick and mud. However, during the rainy season local transportation to the villages and hamlets is by boat. Houses are constructed from bamboo fencing with thatched roofs, so they can be moved to safer areas during the floods.

The majority of people in Netrakona are engaged in agriculture, while the rest work in fishing, rickshaw pulling or labouring. The main crop is rice, which is the staple food, although jute (used for making rope) is also widely cultivated. Agriculture is practised using traditional methods and all members of the family contribute their share. Even the children help in weeding, sowing and harvesting the fields and scaring away the birds, which come to eat rice when it is drying.

Even though low-lying areas are good for rice and fish cultivation, local people are unable to benefit, because 50–80 per cent of land remains flooded for four months during the rainy season. These floods often wash away crops and households, and life comes to a standstill.

A majority of adults do not have any kind of education and are reluctant to send their children to school, as they cannot afford it. Even when families are able to afford schooling, it is the boys who are sent, rather than the girls.



ActionAid has been working with communities in Netrakona since 1983 to provide services in savings and credit, healthcare, family planning and education. For example, ActionAid provides non-formal primary education facilities for young people whose families were unable to send them to school when they were younger.

**The town of Atpara, Netrakrona.**

PHOTO: ELAINE DUIGENAN

**"Before going to school I was afraid of reading and writing and now school for me means a place where I have friends with whom I take lessons from a lovely teacher."**
**Maleka**, a pupil at an ActionAid-funded non-formal primary school

There are also highly popular adult literacy classes for women who are learning to read and write through Reflect. In three years, a total of 834 students have completed the Reflect course and are now able to read, write and do simple calculations, which has resulted in a radical change in their confidence. Consequently, many women have become involved in ActionAid's savings and credit schemes. They come together in groups called *shomitis* to save small amounts and take loans to start small businesses and improve their family incomes.

## Kukri Mukri

Kukri Mukri is an island or *char* in the south of Bangladesh. It lies where the three rivers – the Ganges, Brahmaputra and the Meghna – flow into the Bay of Bengal. Only 6,400 hectares in size, Kukri Mukri is one of Bangladesh's smallest *chars*.

The landscape of Kukri Mukri is flat, traversed by rivers and forested in the north and east. A typical Kukri Mukri scene would include low-lying fertile land, tree-fringed fields, small embankments and an occasional *bari* (a group of small buildings), all criss-crossed by rivers.

Kukri Mukri is just 1m above sea level and flooding is common, as it requires only a small rise in river or tidal levels. This is caused by frequent heavy rains and cyclones. Kukri Mukri lies in the most cyclone-prone area in the world.

To minimise the effects of frequent cyclones in Kukri Mukri, ActionAid helps construct cyclone shelters, which double as primary schools, as well as roads and bridges, allowing people to get to the shelters more quickly. As a result, the cyclone in April 1998 caused far fewer casualties than in previous years.

Kukri Mukri has a population of 10,000. Most people earn a living from fishing and agriculture. However, 80 per cent of the land on Kukri Mukri is owned by fewer than 10 per cent of the people who live there. This means most people are poor and depend on the wealthy for land, employment and loans. However, those with no land depend on erratic earnings as day labourers and many families barely earn enough to feed themselves.

**A river scene in Kukri Mukri.**

PHOTO: LIBA TAYLOR

Trading takes place in small markets or bazaars. Most people sell farm goods such as tea, pulses, potatoes, peppers and livestock, hand-made items such as mats and rope, and fish.

Kukri Mukri is a conservative Muslim area. Gender relations are unequal, so women often cannot take part in political or social life. High value is placed on women working within the home, and employment opportunities for women are scarce, irregular and poorly paid. However, ActionAid has encouraged women to join *shomiti* groups.

Only 20 per cent of the population is literate. Half of the school-going children drop out of primary school before they become literate. ActionAid provides support to primary schools and learning centres in Kukri Mukri, where working adults and children can learn to read and write through Reflect programmes.

**"Literacy training is part of the process. Issues come first and then discussion and action. Then a key word from the discussion, for example the word pani (water) is used as a catalyst to make other words by adding letters. We also teach numeracy skills in the same way. This works very well. Attitudes to education have changed. There is much more enthusiasm now."**

Kaiser Rejve, ActionAid Education Co-ordinator in Kukri Mukri.

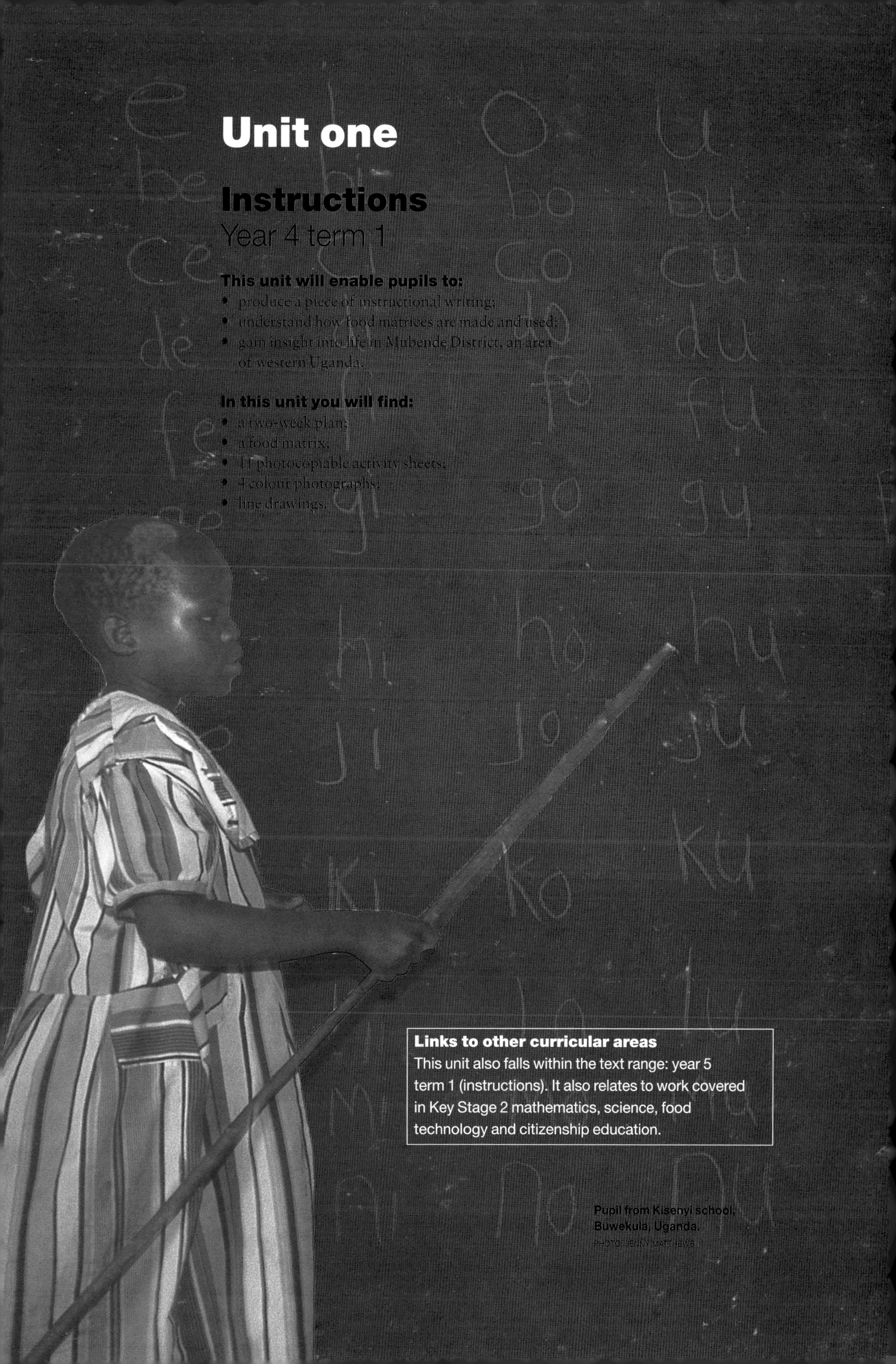

# Unit one

## Instructions

Year 4 term 1

**This unit will enable pupils to:**

- produce a piece of instructional writing;
- understand how food matrices are made and used;
- gain insight into life in Mubende District, an area of western Uganda.

**In this unit you will find:**

- a two-week plan;
- a food matrix;
- 11 photocopiable activity sheets;
- 4 colour photographs;
- line drawings.

**Links to other curricular areas**

This unit also falls within the text range: year 5 term 1 (instructions). It also relates to work covered in Key Stage 2 mathematics, science, food technology and citizenship education.

Pupil from Kisenyi school, Buwekula, Uganda.
PHOTO: JENNY MATTHEWS

# Two-week plan

## Week one

### **Day one** text level 17

**Resources**

Walusimbi's food matrix; activity sheet 1 (Walusimbi's letter – stepped texts 1 to 4)

Look at the food matrix (OHT) and generate questions.

Read out and discuss activity sheet 1 – step 4 (OHT), linking it to the food matrix. Underline the seven action verbs which begin sentences in red, ie *inspect, imagine, draw, write, mark, grant, total.*

Pupils work through the above task, stepping through all four copies of the differentiated texts. These can be stapled together to form a booklet.

Discuss the questions raised in the text, eg '*Do you grow your own food? Consider where our food comes from*'.

**Mathematics afternoon**

Use the food matrix for ranking exercises and drawing graphs.



### **Day two** text level 17, sentence level 3

**Resources**

Photographs 1 and 2; line drawings; activity sheet 1; activity sheet 2 (photocopy to A3)

Read activity sheet 1 – step 4 (OHT). Use photographs 1 and 2 to generate questions.

Identify the seven sentences beginning with the action verbs on activity sheet 1 (OHT). Write these sentences (in the same order) in the instruction boxes on activity sheet 2 (OHT). Match the line drawings with the instructions and show pupils where they would go in the picture boxes.

Pupils perform the above task on their own.

Look at Walusimbi's criteria for choosing his favourite food, eg *easy to grow*. Consider how the pupils' choice of their favourite food would differ from this.

**Example**

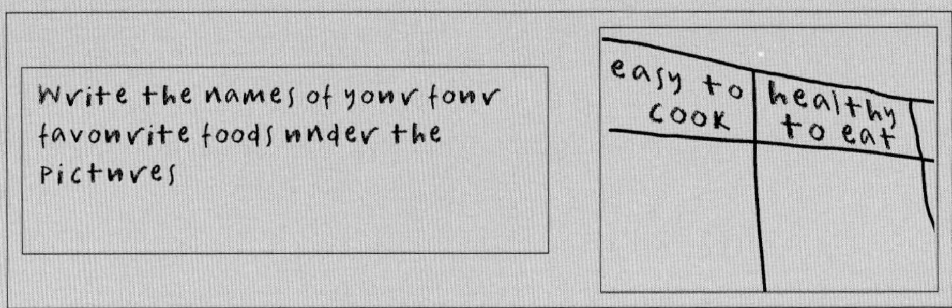

## **Day three** text level 17, sentence level 3

**Resources**

Pupil's activity sheet 2; activity sheet 3 (Action verbs)

Read a pupil's example of activity sheet 2. Consider the use of titles, concise sentences, action verbs and illustrations in instructional writing.

Look at the action verbs on activity sheet 3 (OHT) and clarify their meanings using a dictionary. Match these with their synonyms on activity sheet 2 (OHT) and write them in the larger boxes surrounding the instructions. There can be a range of combinations. Choose a title which encompasses the aim, eg *Seven steps to make a food matrix*.

**Example**

Pupils perform the above task on their own.

Read out the instructions using different action verbs.
Discuss their effectiveness.

## **Day four** text level 22, sentence level 1

**Resources**

Pupil's activity sheet 2; activity sheet 4 (Words to do with time)

Read a pupil's example of activity sheet 2. Consider the use of sequenced steps and temporal connectives in instructional writing.

Look at activity sheet 4 (OHT) and brainstorm other temporal connectives. Add these words (underlined) to the same boxes as the action verbs on activity sheet 2 (OHT). Fill in the equipment used in the correct order, ie *food matrix; pencil*.

**Example**

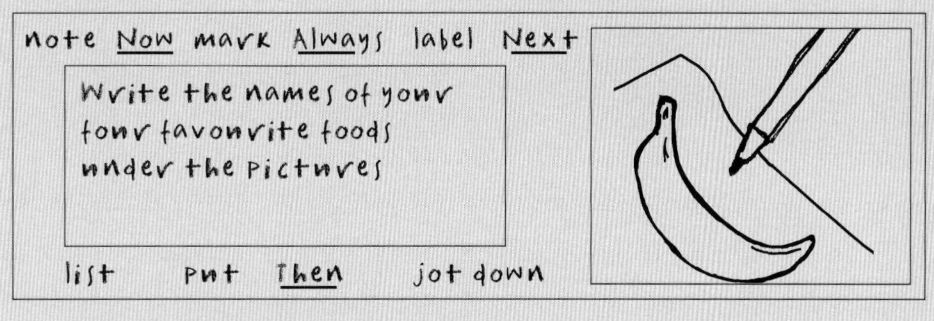


Orally develop sentences using temporal connectives. Choose one temporal connective and one action verb, eg *Next, give each food a score out of ten.*

### **Day five** text level 26, sentence level 1, word level 15

**Resources**

Line drawings; pupil's activity sheet 2; activity sheet 5

Look at activity sheet 5 (OHT), showing the layout of instructional writing as a flow diagram. Consider the use of titles, listing equipment, numbering, sequenced steps and illustrations.

Develop written sentences using the pupil's activity sheet 2 (OHT).

Pupils design a poster on how to make a food matrix for 30 minutes. Using activity sheet 5 is optional. Include a title, equipment, numbers and line drawings and write in joined-up handwriting. Check spellings using a dictionary and display with the food matrix.

**Science afternoon**

Follow the instructions and create food matrices.

## Week two

### **Day six** text level 26, sentence level 1, word level 15

**Resources**

Photographs 3 and 4; activity sheet 6 (How to make *matooke*) – cut up the instructions for sequencing work

Recap features of instructional writing and focus on sequencing. The teacher reads out activity sheet 6 and shows photographs 3 and 4. The pupils listen.

Pupils work in small groups and sequence the jumbled up instructions from activity sheet 6 into the correct order.

Pupils design a recipe card on how to make *matooke* for 30 minutes. Include a title, ingredients, numbers (or bullet points) and write in joined-up handwriting. Check spellings and add to the food matrix display board.

**Food technology afternoon**

Make a *matooke* meal.

### **Day seven** text level 22, sentence level 1

**Resources**

Pupil's recipe cards; activity sheet 7 (Comparing recipes)

Read a pupil's example of a recipe card and recap the layout of instructional writing.

Look at activity sheet 7 (OHT), and discuss the effectiveness of each recipe.

Pupils work in small groups and rank in order of effectiveness their own recipe card and the three others on activity sheet 7. They must decide on five reasons for their choices.

Pupils report their findings to the class.

## **Day eight** text level 22

**Resources**

Activity sheet 8 (How to make a healthy food matrix); activity sheet 9 (Healthy food matrix); activity sheet 10 (Food information)

Read activity sheet 8 (OHT) and recap features of instructional writing.

Follow the instructions on activity sheet 8 (OHT) and use activity sheet 10 (OHT), in order to complete activity sheet 9 (OHT).

Pupils perform the above task on their own.

Volunteers present their completed healthy food matrices to the class.

## **Day nine** sentence level 1

**Resources**

Activity sheet 9, activity sheet 11 (What do you think?)

Look at a pupil's example of activity sheet 9 and generate ideas on how it can be used.

Pupils use activity sheet 9 to complete the questions on activity sheet 11. Divide the class into small groups to consider how to raise awareness of healthy eating. For example, make a leaflet on healthy eating to display in the school dining room or a flyer about growing fruit and vegetables in the school garden. Pupils can develop their ideas in the form of a spider diagram. See example.



**Example**

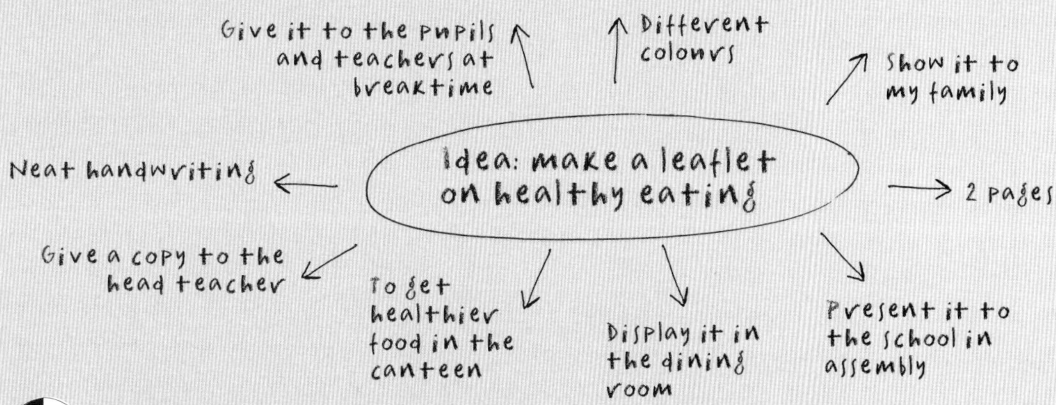


Compare and discuss each group's ideas.

## **Day ten** text level 17, sentence level 1, word level 15

**Resources**

Activity sheets 9–11; examples of pupils' ideas from day nine

Read a pupil's example of ideas from day nine and recap effective ways of designing non-fiction texts, eg titles, bullet points and concise sentences.

Design the outline of a leaflet, flyer or poster, using information from activity sheets 9, 10 and 11 and the pupil's ideas from day nine.

Pupils design an information text on the importance of healthy eating for 30 minutes. This should be written in neat joined-up handwriting and used to implement day nine's ideas for action.

# Activity sheet • Walusimbi's food matrix

| Favourite foods | Easy to grow | Easy to cook | Healthy to eat | Total |
|---|---|---|---|---|
|  *Matooke* (Green bananas) | 8 | 9 | 9 | 26 |
|  Groundnuts | 3 | 7 | 9 | 19 |
| 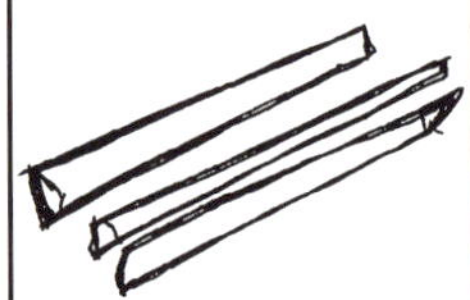 Sugar cane | 6 | 10 | 7 | 23 |
|  Maize flour | 5 | 6 | 9 | 20 |

**Lulagala Village**
**Uganda**

Dear class,

Hello. My name is Walusimbi. I am ten years old. I live on a farm in Lulagala Village in Uganda.

I am writing to show you how to make a food matrix. Here is the first point. Look at the food matrix and get a pencil to fill it in.

Think of your favourite foods. I chose *matooke*, groundnuts, sugar cane and maize flour. These are crops grown on my parents' farm. My sisters and I help my parents on the farm. It is hard work.

Next is the third point. Make pictures of your favourite foods in the food column.

Jot down the names of your four favourite foods under the pictures.

Now the fifth point. Put three reasons why these are your favourite foods on the top row of the food matrix. I wrote these foods are easy to grow, easy to cook and healthy to eat. Give each food a score out of ten. 

Finally is the seventh point. Add up the total for each food and write it on the food matrix. You can compare the answers with your friends.

Groundnuts are the hardest to grow. Do you grow your own food? Maize flour is the hardest to cook. We use a lot of firewood to cook maize flour. Do you use firewood to cook?

*Matooke* is my favourite food. I eat it for three months of the year when it is ripe. When do you eat your favourite food?

I often sing this song:

Food gives us energy, food makes us grow, food gives us health.

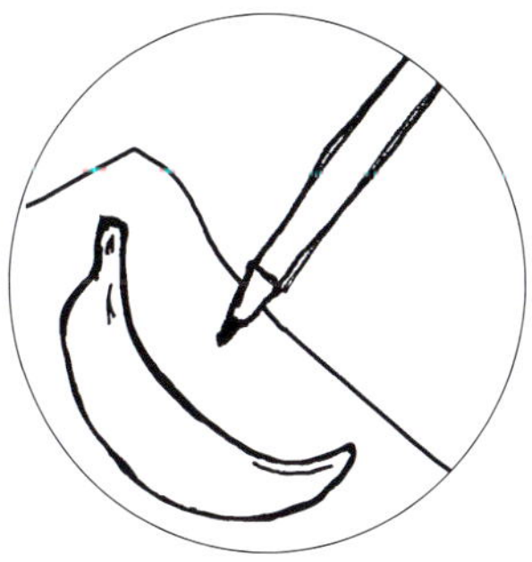

I hope you have enjoyed reading my letter.

From Walusimbi

# Activity sheet 1 step 2 • Walusimbi's letter

Lulagala Village
Uganda

Dear class,

Hello. My name is Walusimbi and I am ten years old. I live on a farm in Lulagala Village in Uganda. From my house I can see beautiful hills and valleys.

Food is an important part of our lives in Lulagala Village. I am writing to show you how to make a food matrix. Here is the first point. Study the food matrix and get a pencil to fill it in.

Think of your favourite foods. I chose *matooke*, groundnuts, sugar cane and maize flour. These are crops grown on my parents' farm. My sisters and I help my parents every day. It is hard work.

Next is the third point. Make pictures of your favourite foods in the food column. Write the names of your four favourite foods under the pictures.

Now the fifth point. Mark the top row with three reasons why these are your favourite foods. I wrote these foods are easy to grow, easy to cook and healthy to eat. Give each food a score out of ten. Ten is the highest and one is the lowest.

Finally the seventh point. Add up the total for each food and write it on the food matrix. You can compare the answers with your friends.

Groundnuts are the hardest food to grow. *Matooke* is the easiest food to grow. Do you grow your own food? Maize flour is the hardest to cook. It takes a long time to cook and uses a lot of firewood. Do you use firewood to cook?

*Matooke* is my favourite food. I can only eat *matooke* for three months of the year when it is ripe. When do you eat your favourite food?

I enjoy eating food and often sing this song:

Food gives us energy, food makes us grow, food gives us health.

I hope you have enjoyed reading my letter.

From Walusimbi

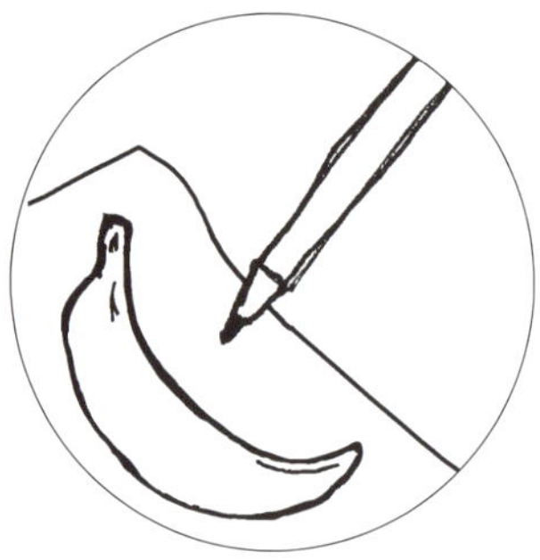

# Activity sheet 1 step 3 • Walusimbi's letter

Lulagala Village
Mubende District
Uganda

Dear class,

Hello. My name is Walusimbi and I am ten years old. I live on a farm in Lulagala Village in Uganda. Lulagala Village is in Mubende District in the west of Uganda. From my house I can see beautiful hills and valleys.

Food is an important part of our lives in Lulagala Village. I am writing to explain how to make a food matrix. Here is the first point. Study the food matrix and get a pencil to fill it in. It shows interesting information about the food people eat.

Imagine your favourite foods. I chose *matooke*, groundnuts, sugar cane and maize flour. These are crops grown on my family's farm. My sisters and I spend many hours every day helping my parents. It is difficult work.

Next is the third point. Draw pictures of your favourite foods in the food column on the food matrix. Write the names of your four favourite foods under the pictures. Now the fifth point. Mark the top row with three reasons why these are your favourite foods. My reasons are because these foods are easy to grow, easy to cook and healthy to eat. Give each food a score out of ten. Ten is the highest and one is the lowest.



Finally is the seventh point. Add up the total for each food and write it on the food matrix. You can compare it with your friends.

Groundnuts are the hardest to grow and *matooke* is the easiest. I wonder if you grow your own food. Maize flour had the lowest mark in the easy to cook column. This is because it takes a long time to cook and it uses a lot of firewood. We don't like using a lot of firewood because we have to cut down trees. Do you use firewood to cook?

*Matooke* is my favourite food and it scored the highest mark. I eat *matooke* for three months of the year after it is harvested. When do you eat your favourite food?

I enjoy eating food and often sing this song on the way to school:

*Emmere etuwa amaangi, emmere etuyamba okukul, emmere etuwa obulama*

(Food gives us energy, food makes us grow, food gives us health).

I hope you have enjoyed reading my letter.

Best wishes from Walusimbi

# Activity sheet 1 step 4 • Walusimbi's letter

**Lulagala Village**
**Mubende District**
**Uganda**

Dear class,

Hello. My name is Walusimbi and I am ten years old. I live on a farm in Lulagala Village in Mubende District in the west of Uganda. From my house I can see beautiful rolling hills and green valleys.

Food is an important part of our lives in Lulagala Village and I am writing to explain how to make a food matrix. Here is the first point. Inspect the food matrix and get a pencil to fill it in. It shows fascinating information about the food people eat.

Imagine your four favourite foods. I chose *matooke*, groundnuts, sugar cane and maize flour. These are crops grown on my family's farm and my sisters and I spend several hours every day helping my parents. It is demanding work.

Next is the third point. Draw pictures of your favourite foods in the food column of the food matrix. Write the names of your four favourite foods under the pictures. Now the fifth point. Mark the top row with three reasons why these are your favourite foods. My reasons are because these foods are easy to grow, easy to cook and healthy to eat. Grant each food a score out of ten. Ten is the highest and one is the lowest.



Finally is the seventh point. Total the marks for each food and write them on the food matrix. When you have worked out which food comes first, second, third and fourth you can compare it with your friends.

Groundnuts are the hardest to grow and *matooke* is the easiest. I wonder if you grow your own food. Sugar cane scored ten in the easy to cook column because we don't have to cook it! Maize flour scored the lowest because it takes a long time to cook and uses a lot of firewood. We try not to use too much firewood because it means cutting down trees and we want to protect our environment. Do you use firewood to cook?

*Matooke* is my favourite food and it scored the highest total mark. We eat *matooke* for three months of the year after it is harvested. I love this time of year. Do you have to wait for certain times in the year to eat your favourite food?

I enjoy eating food and often sing this little song every morning on the way to school:

*Emmere etuwa amaangi, emmere etuyamba okuku, emmere etuwa obulama*

(Food gives us energy, food makes us grow, food gives us health).

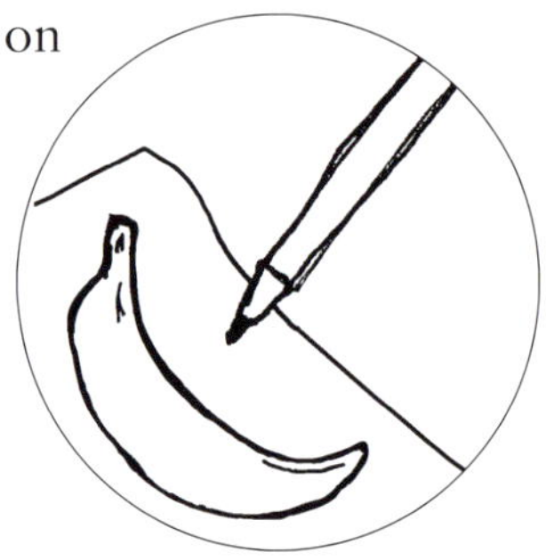

I hope you have enjoyed reading my letter and understand more about food in Uganda.

Best wishes from Walusimbi

# Activity sheet 2

Title ______________________ Equipment ______________________

| Instruction | Picture |
|---|---|
| | |
| | |
| | |
| | |
| | |
| | |
| | |

# Activity sheet 3 • Action verbs

note 

grant

study 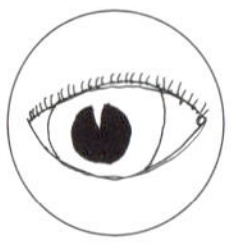

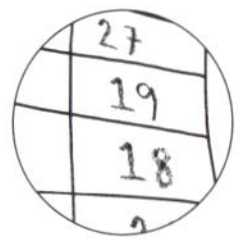 count up

 make

mark 

award

put

draw

think of 

inspect

sketch

list

imagine 

give 

 jot down

label

examine

 consider

add up

write

look at 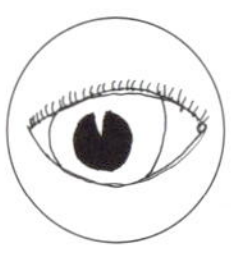

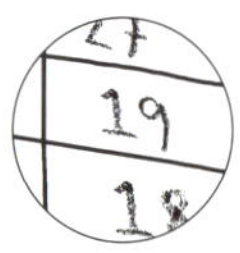 total

# Activity sheet 4 • Words to do with time

**Then**

**First**

**After this**

**Always**

**Now**

**Next**



**Finally**

**Thirdly**

**Secondly**

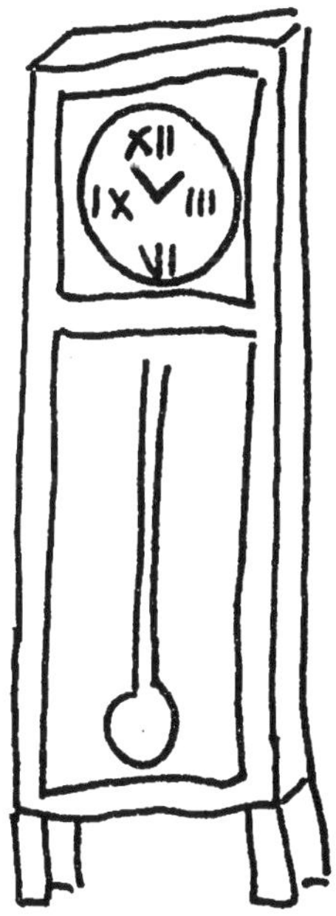

# Activity sheet 5

Title ______________________________

Equipment ______________________________

| Number | Instruction | Picture |
| --- | --- | --- |
| | | |
| | ↓ | |
| | | |
| | ↓ | |
| | | |
| | ↓ | |
| | | |
| | ↓ | |
| | | |
| | ↓ | |
| | | |
| | ↓ | |
| | | |

## Line drawings

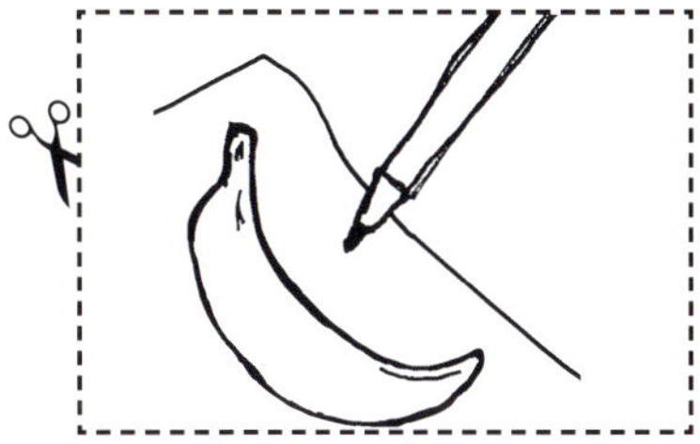

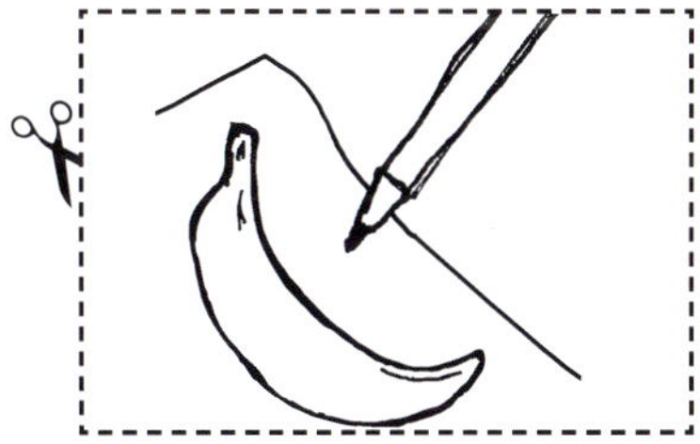

## Activity sheet 6 • How to make *matooke*

This recipe serves four people.

**Ingredients**
10 *matooke* (green bananas)
one handful of green *matooke* leaves
20mm of water

**Method**

First, collect the *matooke* and their leaves.

Secondly, peel the *matooke*.

Next, wrap the *matooke* in the leaves.

Always put the *matooke* and the leaves in a saucepan.

Then pour the water into the saucepan.

Now place the lid on the saucepan.

Afterwards, cook it for one hour.

Finally, mash the *matooke* and serve it.

**1**

## A recipe for making *matooke*

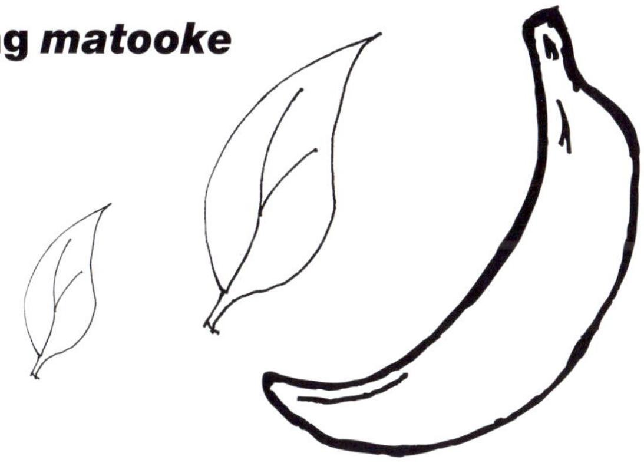

What you need

- *Matooke*
- *Matooke* leaves
- Water

What you do

- You get some *matooke* and peel them.
- You wrap them in their leaves.
- You put them in a saucepan with the water.
- You cook them until they are ready and mash them.

**2**

## *Matooke*

Collect some *matooke* and some leaves. Cook them together in a saucepan for an hour. The *matooke* is ready.



**3**

Making *Matooke*

- Serves four people

Ingredients

- 10 *matooke*
- A handful of green *matooke* leaves
- 20mm of water

Equipment

- 1 saucepan

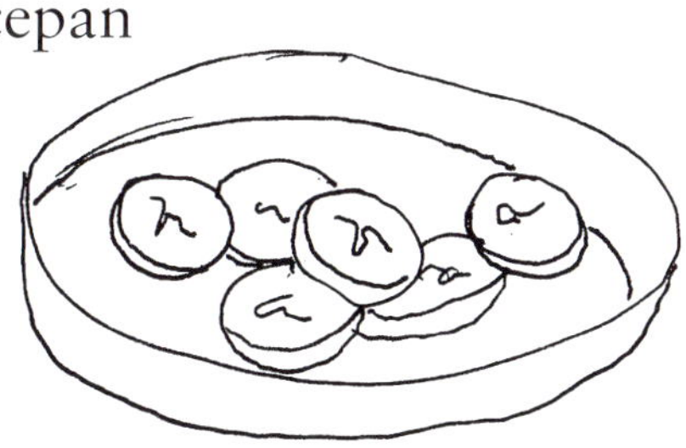

Method

- Gather the *matooke* and the leaves.
- Peel the *matooke*.
- Wrap the *matooke* in the leaves.
- Put the *matooke* and the leaves in the saucepan.
- Pour the water into the saucepan.
- Place the lid on the saucepan
- Cook it for one hour.
- Mash the *matooke*.
- Serve it.

# Activity sheet 8 • How to make a healthy food matrix

Children from Mubende District in Uganda are very good at making food matrices. Below they tell us how to make a healthy food matrix. Let's see if we can follow their instructions.

**1** First, think of seven foods you eat most often.

**2** Secondly, sketch pictures of the foods you eat most often in the 'Food' column of the healthy food matrix.

**3** Thirdly, write the names of the foods you eat most often under the pictures in your neatest, joined-up handwriting.

**4** Next, label the top row with these types of food:

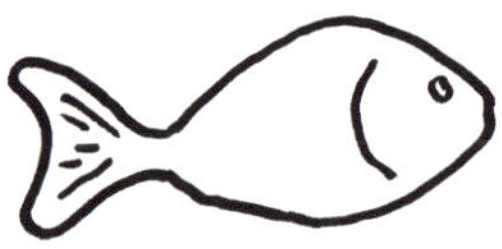

Bread, cereal, potatoes and rice

Fruit and vegetables

Meat, fish and beans

Milk and dairy foods

Fat

Sugar

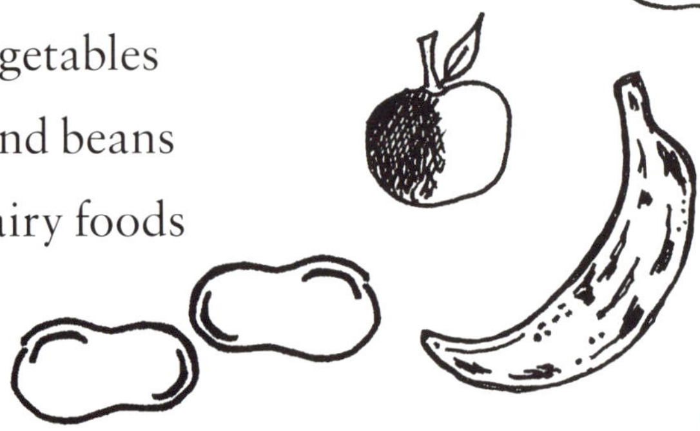

**5** After this, tick one box for each food, eg tick the 'sugar' box for 'chocolate'.

**6** Finally, total the number of ticks for each food class and write it in the bottom row.

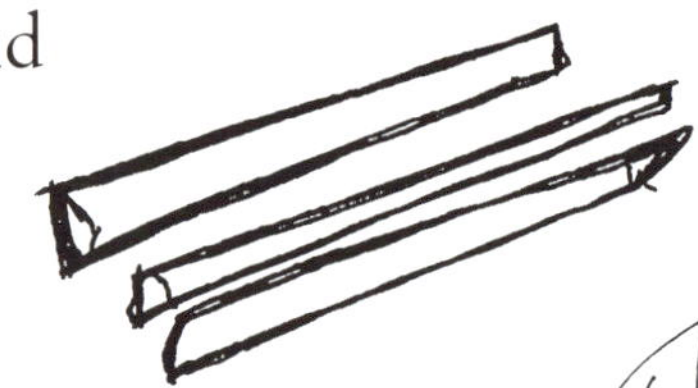

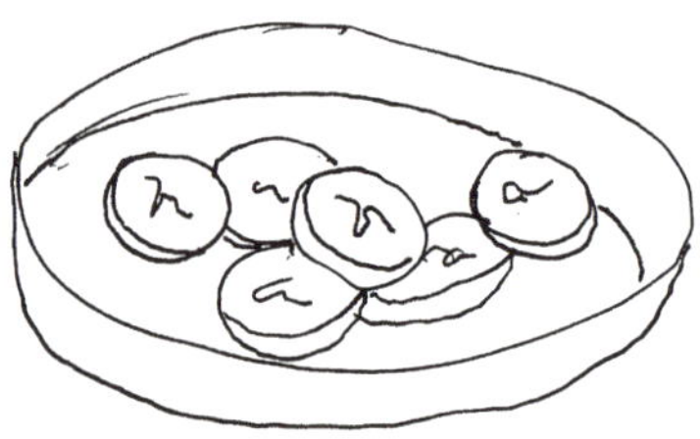

# Activity sheet 9 • Healthy food matrix

| **Food** | Bread cereal potatoes and rice | | | | | |
|---|---|---|---|---|---|---|
| | | | | | | |
| | | | | | | |
| | | | | | | |
| | | | | | | |
| | | | | | | |
| | | | | | | |
| | | | | | | |
| **Total** | | | | | | |

# Activity sheet 10 • Healthy food information

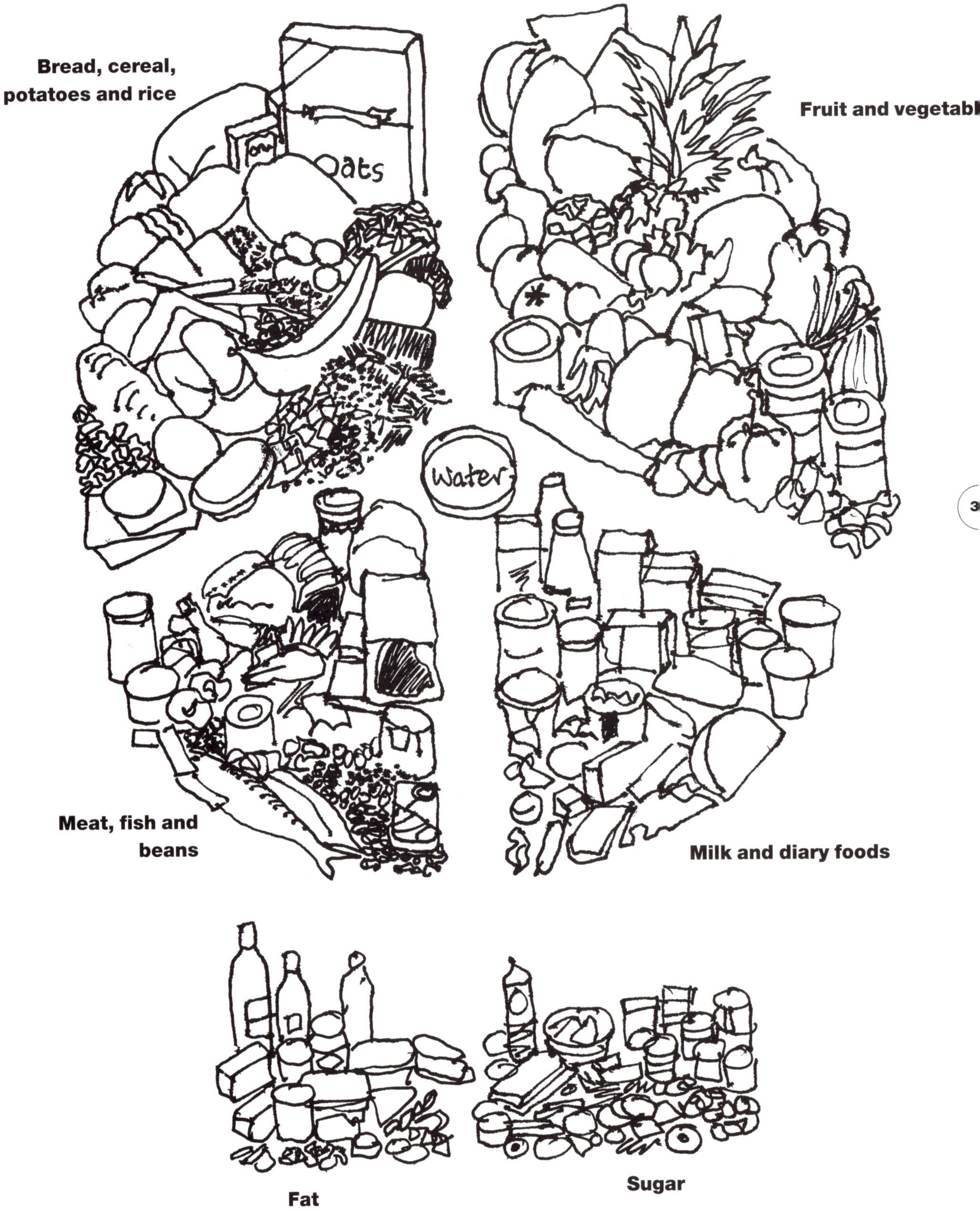

## Activity sheet 11 • What do you think?

Which type of food do you eat most often? ______________________

Which type of food do you eat least often? ______________________

Do you eat all types of food? (yes or no) ______________________

**Are these sentences true or false?**

Sheep lay eggs. ______________________

Taking lots of exercise is fun and very important. ______________________

You should eat five pieces of fruit and vegetables every day. ______________________

Eating pizza helps you see in the dark. ______________________

It is good to eat a mixture of all types of food. ______________________

Sticky chewy sweets cause tooth decay. ______________________

Spaghetti grows on trees. ______________________

It is better to eat less fat and sugar. ______________________

Do you eat enough healthy food? (yes or no) ______________________

What types of food do you need to eat more of? ______________________

What types of food do you need to eat less of? ______________________

How can you tell other people about healthy eating?

______________________________________________

______________________

______________________

# Unit two

## Non-chronological report

Year 5 term 2

**This unit will enable pupils to:**

- produce a piece of report writing;
- understand how to make and use natural resource maps;
- gain insight into life in Mubende District, an area of western Uganda.

**In this unit you will find:**

- a two-week plan;
- 2 natural resource maps;
- 10 photocopiable activity sheets;
- 4 colour photographs;
- line drawings.

**Links to other curricular areas**

This text also falls within the text range: year 6 term 1 and year 6 term 3 (non-chronological report). It also relates to work covered in Key Stage 2 geography, history, English, art, IT and citizenship education.

**Children from Llangattock Church in Wales Primary School, Powys, UK.**

PHOTO: LIZ THOMAS

# Two-week plan

## Week one

### Day one text level 17

**Resources**

1970 natural resource map; activity sheet 1 (Katonga Village in 1970 – stepped texts 1 to 4); activity sheet 3 (Katonga Village in 1970 and 2000 – photocopy to A3)

Look at the 1970 natural resource map (OHT) and match the nouns with the symbols on the map.

Read out and discuss activity sheet 1 – step 4 (OHT). Consider the impersonal style of non-chronological reports. Underline the nouns from the natural resource map in blue. Identify one or two facts about each noun, eg *river – provided water for cooking, cleaning and irrigating crops* and *wild animals – lived in the woodland*. Add this information to activity sheet 3 (OHT) next to the appropriate symbols.

Pupils perform the above task on their own, stepping through all four copies of the differentiated texts. These can be stapled together to form a booklet.

Read out the facts and relate to the 1970 natural resource map.



### Day two text level 17

**Resources**

Photographs 5, 6, 7 and 8; 2000 natural resource map; activity sheet 2 (Katonga Village in 2000 – stepped texts 1 to 4); activity sheet 3

Look at photographs 5, 6, 7 and 8 and generate questions about the area, eg What crops do people grow in the area? Follow day one's guidelines, using the 2000 natural resource map (OHT), activity sheet 2 and activity sheet 3.

**History afternoon**

Interview parents, teachers and other adults in the community about how their local environment has changed over the past 30 years. Focus on pollution, eg *traffic and river pollution, and the loss of open space*. Find out what has been done to improve the situation, eg *cycle paths, tree planting schemes*. Try to find old pictures /newspapers from your local library.

## **Day three** text level 17, sentence level 3

### Resources

1970 and 2000 natural resource maps; activity sheet 3; activity sheet 4 (Statement banks)

Study the two natural resource maps (OHT) and identify similarities and differences between them. Consider the use of detailed statements in non-chronological reports.

Read activity sheet 4 (OHT) and write the statements next to the correct symbol on activity sheet 3 (OHT).

Pupils perform the above task on their own.

Discuss the differences between Katonga Village in 1970 and 2000.

### Geography afternoon

Use photographs 5, 6, 7 and 8 and the information about Katonga Village in 2000 on activity sheet 3 to describe the area.

## **Day four** text level 21, sentence level 8

### Resources

Line drawings; activity sheet 3; activity sheet 5 (Comparing Katonga Village – photocopy to A3)



Read out and discuss a pupil's example of activity sheet 3. Consider the use of comparisons in non-chronological reports.

Choose one fact from each of the six 1970 sections of activity sheet 3 and match it with a corresponding fact from the six 2000 sections. Write this information on activity sheet 5 (OHT), choose a comparative word or phrase and add the line drawings. There are at least 30 combinations. See example.

### Example

| | | | |
|---|---|---|---|
| in 1970 | birds nested in areas near the houses. (A similarity is) | in 2000 | birds nested in areas away from the houses. |
| in 1970 | there were 5 houses (whereas) | in 2000 | there were 16 houses. |

Pupils perform the above task on their own.

Read out and discuss the comparison sentences.

### Geography afternoon

Discuss the following statements:

- People who eat chocolate may never have seen a cacao tree and people who grow the cocoa may never have eaten chocolate.
- Fifty Kit-Kats are eaten every second of the day, but high sales don't always help the cocoa farmers.
- During the past 10 years the price of a chocolate bar has gone up by two thirds and the price of cocoa has gone down by half. So it's the chocolate companies and not the cocoa farmers who are making the profit.
- If you buy fairly traded chocolate it guarantees cocoa farmers in countries like Uganda are paid a good price for their cocoa. Look out for the Fairtrade logo.

Guarentees a better deal for Third World Producers Fairtrade

## Day five text level 22, sentence level 8, word level 1

**Resources**

Line drawings; activity sheet 5

Consider the layout of non-chronological reports. Focus on the use of titles, illustrations and captions.

Write out the six comparative sentences from activity sheet 5 and think of other combinations. Choose a title, eg *Changes in Katonga Village over 30 years* and captions for the line drawings, eg *A health centre in Katonga Village*.

Pupils write a non-chronological report comparing Katonga Village in 1970 with 2000 for 30 minutes. Include a title, detailed sentences, comparison words, illustrations and captions. Check spellings and display with the natural resource maps.

**Geography afternoon**

Recap changes in Katonga Village between 1970 and 2000. Draw a table showing the advantages and disadvantages of 1970 and 2000 and vote on where pupils would prefer to live and why.

# Week two



## Day six

Consider the meanings of natural and human resources and brainstorm examples of these in the school playground.

Draw an outline map of the school and label the natural resources in one colour, eg *hedgerow; grass area; oak tree; flowers* and the human resources in another colour, eg *science block; sports hall; concrete playground; litter bins*. Next to each resource write a detailed fact, eg *Sports Hall – It has white walls and no windows*. Give the map a title, eg *A map showing our school environment*. Make a key to show the natural and human resources.

Pupils perform the above task in small groups.

Groups present their maps to the class.

## Day seven

**Resources**

Pupil's school environment map

Look at a pupil's school environment map and generate questions.

Create a symbol to represent litter, eg ✱ and mark places where litter is dropped on the map. Add the symbol to the key. Discuss how to improve the litter situation, eg *extra bins; signs*. Create symbols to represent these improvements, mark them on the map and add them to the key. See example.

**Example**

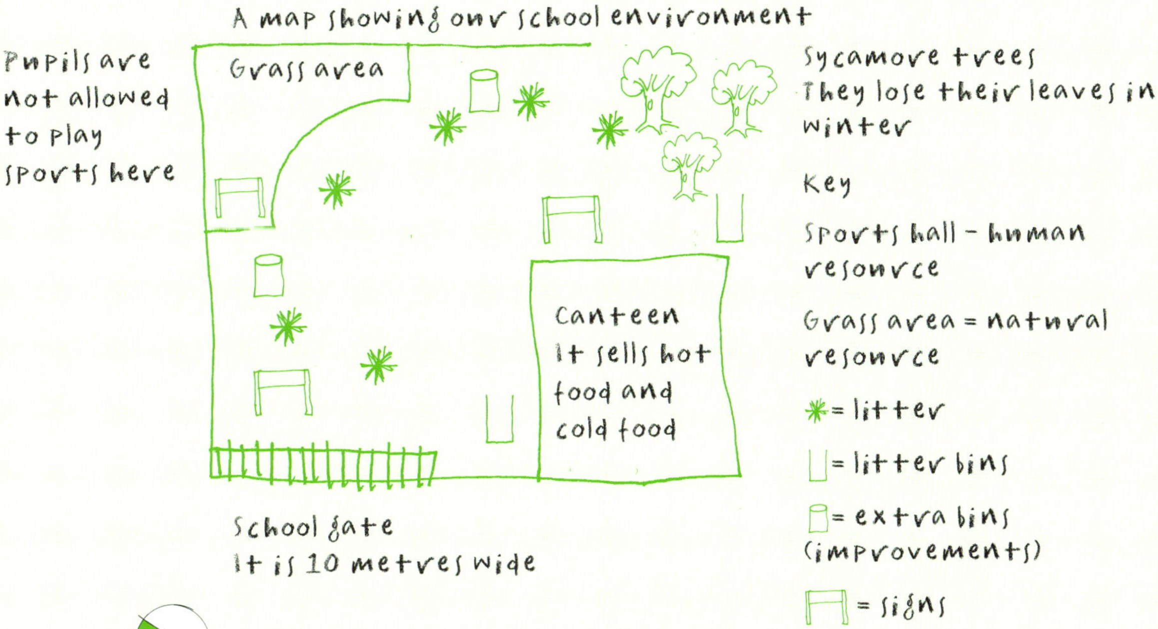


Pupils perform the above task in small groups.

Groups present their maps to the class.

## Day eight text level 16

**Resources**

Activity sheet 6 (Don't bin it – save it!); activity sheet 7 (Think before you bin it!)

Read activity sheet 6 (OHT) and look at activity sheet 7 (OHT).

Identify the six items in the rubbish bin on activity sheet 7 (OHT) and underline these in blue on activity sheet 6 (OHT). Underline the material each item is made from in red and a way in which it can be recycled in black. Add this information to the chart on activity sheet 7 (OHT). See example.

**Example**

| | | |
|---|---|---|
| sketch pad | paper | paper can be recycled in paper banks |

Pupils perform the above task on their own.

Read out and discuss answers.

**English/art afternoon**

Write a letter, make a petition or design a poster highlighting the importance of recycling in school and use it.

## Day nine text level 21

**Resources**

Activity sheet 8 (Are you environmentally friendly?); activity sheet 9 (Being environmentally friendly)

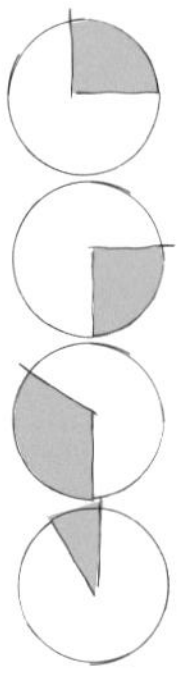

Look at activity sheet 8 (OHT). Consider the use of factual information based on surveys in non-chronological reports.

Discuss and fill in activity sheet 8 (OHT). Use this to complete activity sheet 9 (OHT).

Pupils perform the above task on their own.

Read out and discuss answers.

**IT afternoon**

Look at a range of websites and the ways in which information is presented, eg www.eia-international.org.uk

## Day ten text level 24, sentence level 3, word level 1

**Resources**

Pupil's work from week two; activity sheet 10 (Proof-reading marks)

Consider the layout of websites that report factual information. Focus on the use of titles, maps, charts and detailed facts.

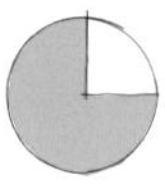

Pupils design a website on paper that reports information about recycling and their school environment for 45 minutes. Include their school environment maps and information from activity sheets 7, 8 and 9. Use activity sheet 10 to proof-read sentences.

# A natural resource map of Katonga Village in 1970

Match these nouns with the symbols on the map:

**houses** **river** **fish** **trees**

**wild animals** **herbs** **wild birds**

Katonga Village is an imaginary village in Uganda

## A natural resource map of Katonga Village in 2000

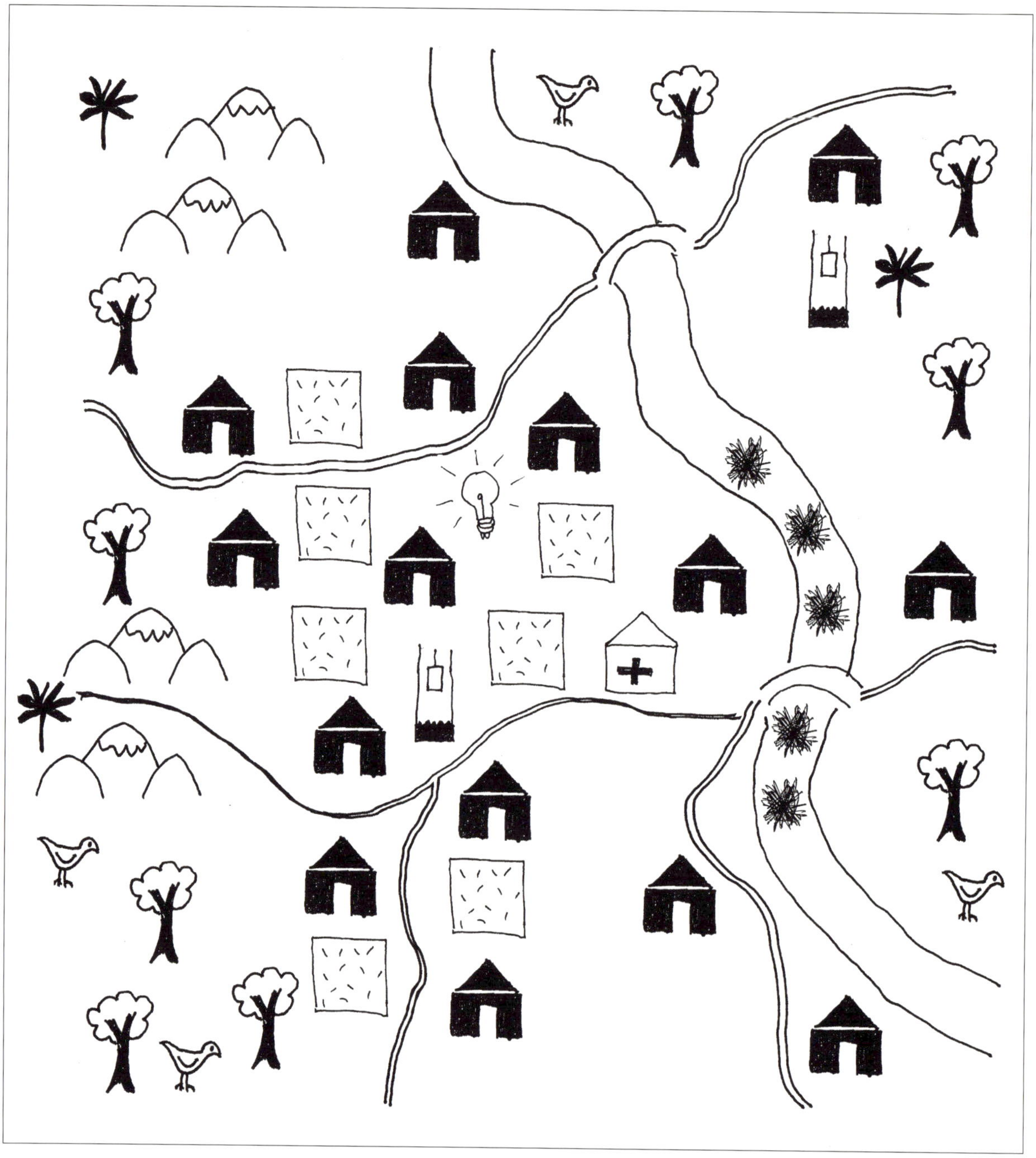

Match these nouns with the symbols on the map:

| | | | |
|---|---|---|---|
| **houses** | **river** | **rubbish** | **trees** |
| **fields** | **herbs** | **wild birds** | **wells** |
| **electricity** | **health centre** | | |

Katonga Village is an imaginary village in Uganda

Katonga is a village in Uganda. There are mountains, hills and valleys in the area around the village. In 1970 the people lived in houses next to a river and alongside a road. A river ran through Katonga Village. The river water was used for cooking, cleaning and watering crops.

*A baobab tree*

Trees grew everywhere. There were baobab trees. Crops were grown amongst the trees. Herbs such as rosy periwinkle also grew amongst the trees.

In the woodland wild animals lived – for example, wart hogs, which are wild pigs. In the area there were many wild birds – for example, eagles and herons.

# Activity sheet 1 step 2 • Katonga Village in 1970

Katonga is a village in the west of Uganda. It is surrounded by mountains, hills and valleys. In 1970 the people lived in houses next to a river and alongside a narrow road. The roads led into the woodland.

A river ran through Katonga Village. This provided water for cooking, cleaning and watering crops. People ate fish from the river.

Trees grew everywhere. There were banana trees and baobab trees. Crops were grown amongst the trees and these included groundnuts and *matooke* (green bananas). Herbs such as rosy periwinkle also grew amongst the trees.

Wild animals also lived in the woodland. These included wart hogs, howler monkeys, tree frogs and butterflies. Wart hogs are wild pigs.

Eagles and yellow weaver birds nested in the trees and could be seen everywhere. Herons lived along the river banks.

*A baobab tree*

Katonga is a village situated in the west of Uganda. It was surrounded by mountains, rolling hills and shallow, swampy valleys. In 1970 the people lived in houses next to a river and alongside narrow roads. The roads led into the woodland, but when it rained they became very muddy and difficult to travel on.

A river ran through Katonga Village. This provided water for cooking, cleaning and irrigating crops. People ate fish from the river.

Trees grew everywhere. There were banana trees, wild oil palm trees, acacia trees and baobab trees. Crops were grown amongst the trees and these included groundnuts, *matooke* (green bananas), mangoes and pineapples. Herbs such as rosy periwinkle also grew amongst the trees.

Wild animals lived in the woodland. These included wart hogs, howler monkeys, tree frogs and swallow-tailed butterflies. Wart hogs, which are wild pigs, roamed around the woodland.

Eagles and yellow weaver birds nested in the trees and could be seen everywhere. Flamingos and herons lived along the river banks.

*A baobab tree*

# Activity sheet 1 step 4 • Katonga Village in 1970

Katonga is a village situated in Mubende District in the west of Uganda. In 1970 it was surrounded by rolling hills and shallow, swampy valleys and was covered in green woodland.

The people lived in houses next to a river and alongside narrow roads. The roads led into the woodland, but when it rained they became very muddy and difficult to travel on. Katonga Village was very remote.

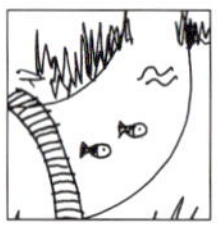

A river ran through Katonga Village. This provided water for cooking, cleaning and irrigating crops. People also ate a variety of fish from the river.

Trees grew everywhere. There were banana trees, wild oil palm trees, flat-topped acacia trees and wide-trunked baobab trees. Crops were grown amongst the trees and these included groundnuts, cassava, sesame, *matooke* (green bananas), mangoes and pineapples. Herbs such as rosy periwinkle also grew amongst the trees and were used as medicines.

Wild animals lived in the woodland. These included wart hogs, howler monkeys, tree frogs and swallow-tailed butterflies. Wart hogs, which are wild pigs, roamed around the woodland. They have tufted tails that stick up in the air like antennae.

Eagles and yellow weaver birds nested in the trees and could be seen everywhere. Flamingos, herons and storks lived along the river banks and waded at the water's edge.

*A baobab tree*

# Activity sheet 2 step 1 • Katonga Village in 2000

*A cacao tree and cocoa beans*

Katonga is a village in Uganda. There are hills and valleys in the area. There are villages and towns too. Most houses in Katonga Village have electricity. The houses are near a river, roads and mountains.

A river runs through Katonga Village. The river water is used for watering crops. There is rubbish in the river. People often clear the rubbish from the river. People get clean water from wells.

Trees are being cut down in Katonga Village. Cutting down trees is a problem all over the world.

Crops such as coffee, cocoa and sugar are grown in fields. Some cocoa is sold to other countries and made into chocolate.

People use herbs and modern medicines when they are ill. There is a health centre in Katonga Village.

Wild animals do not live in the area. People own cows, goats and chickens. Yellow weaver birds can be seen everywhere.

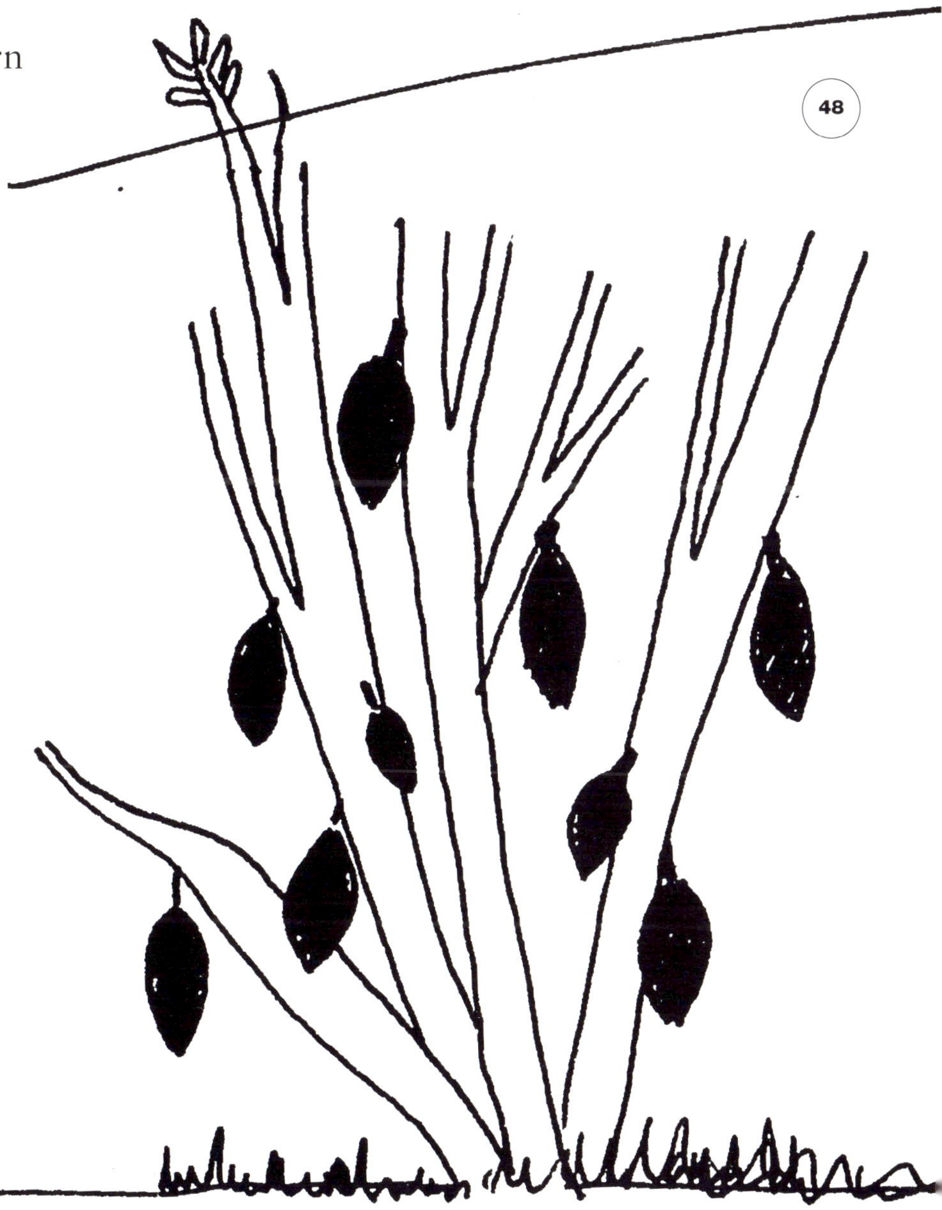

## Activity sheet 2 step 2 • Katonga Village in 2000

*A cacao tree and cocoa beans*

Katonga is a village in the west of Uganda. It is surrounded by hills and valleys. There are several villages and towns in the area.

Most houses in Katonga Village have electricity. Houses cover a huge area. They are near a river, roads and mountains. The roads are made of tarmac.

A river runs through Katonga village. This provides water for watering crops. There is rubbish in the river. People are often seen clearing rubbish from the river. People get safe, clean water from the wells.

Trees are being cut down in Katonga Village. This is because people need more space to grow crops. Cutting down trees is a problem all over the world. The people of Katonga Village have decided to plant more trees.

Crops such as coffee, cocoa, sugar and tea are grown in fields. Some cocoa is sold to other countries where it is made into chocolate.

People use herbs and modern medicines when they are ill. There is a health centre in Katonga Village.

Wild animals do not live in the area next to Katonga Village. People own cows, goats and chickens. Yellow weaver birds can be seen everywhere. They nest in the trees and fly into the village.

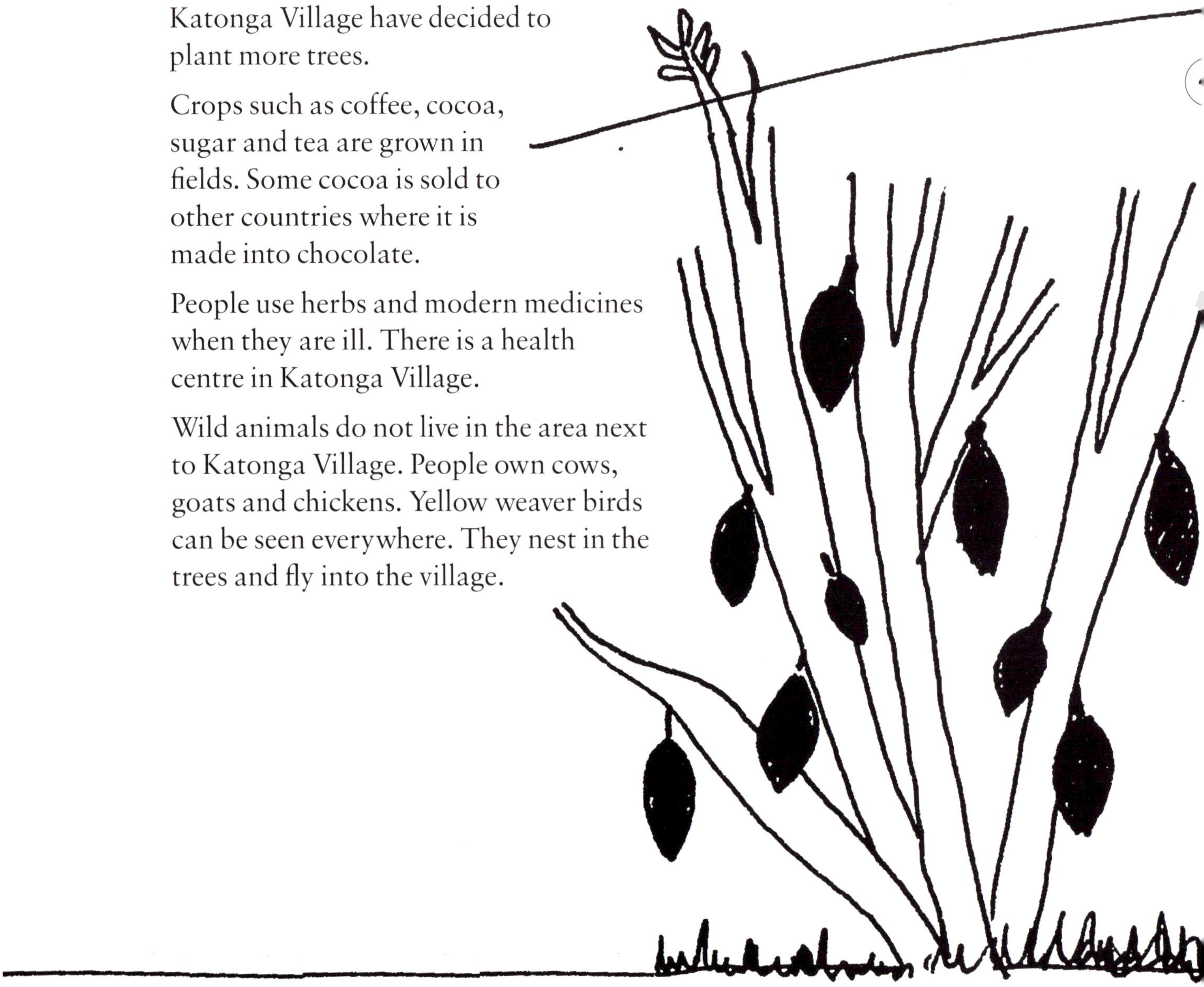

# Activity sheet 2 step 3 • Katonga Village in 2000

Katonga is a large village situated in the west of Uganda. It is surrounded by rolling hills and shallow, swampy valleys. There are several villages and towns in the area.

Most houses in Katonga Village have electricity. Houses cover a large area near a river, wide roads and mountains. The roads lead to other villages and towns. Many people own minibuses called *matatus* and drive passengers to markets.

*A cacao tree and cocoa beans*

A river runs through Katonga Village. This provides water for irrigating crops. There is pollution in the river and people are worried about it. People are often seen clearing rubbish from the river.

Wells are found in Katonga Village and these provide safe, clean water from under the ground.

Trees are being cut down in Katonga Village. This is because the population needs more space for crops. Cutting down trees is a problem all over the world. The people of Katonga Village have decided to plant some fast growing trees.

Crops such as coffee, cocoa, sugar, tea and cotton are grown in fields and sold in markets. Some cocoa is sold to other countries where it is made into chocolate. Not many people in Katonga Village have tasted chocolate because it is very expensive.

People use herbs and modern medicines when they are ill. There is a health centre in Katonga Village and a hospital in the area.

Wild animals do not live in the area next to Katonga Village. People own cows, goats and chickens, which provide meat, milk and eggs. Yellow weaver birds can be seen flying everywhere. They nest in the trees and fly into the village, chirping loudly.

# Activity sheet 2 step 4 • Katonga Village in 2000

Katonga is a sizeable village located in Mubende District in the west of Uganda. It is surrounded by rolling hills and shallow, swampy valleys. Villages and towns are scattered throughout the area.

*A cacao tree and cocoa beans*

Most houses in Katonga Village have electricity. They cover a large area near a river, wide roads and high mountains. The roads are made of tarmac and lead to other villages and towns. Many people own minibuses called *matatus* and drive passengers to markets, where they buy and sell food.

A river runs through Katonga Village. This provides water for irrigating crops. There is pollution in the river and many people are worried about it. Volunteers are often seen clearing the rubbish from the river. Wells are found in Katonga Village and these provide safe, clean water from deep underground.

Trees are being cut down in Katonga Village. This is because the population needs more land for crops and more timber for firewood and making houses. Cutting down trees is a problem all over the world and the people of Katonga Village have decided to plant fast growing trees for future generations to use.

Crops such as coffee, cocoa, sugar, tea and cotton are grown in fields and sold in markets. Some cocoa is sold to other countries where it is made into chocolate. Not many people in Katonga Village have tasted chocolate because it is an expensive luxury.

People use a combination of herbs and modern medicines when they are ill. There is a health centre in Katonga Village and a hospital in the nearest town.

Wild animals do not live in the area next to Katonga Village. People own cows, goats and chickens, which provide meat, milk and eggs. Yellow weaver birds can be seen everywhere. They nest in the trees and fly into the village, chirping loudly.

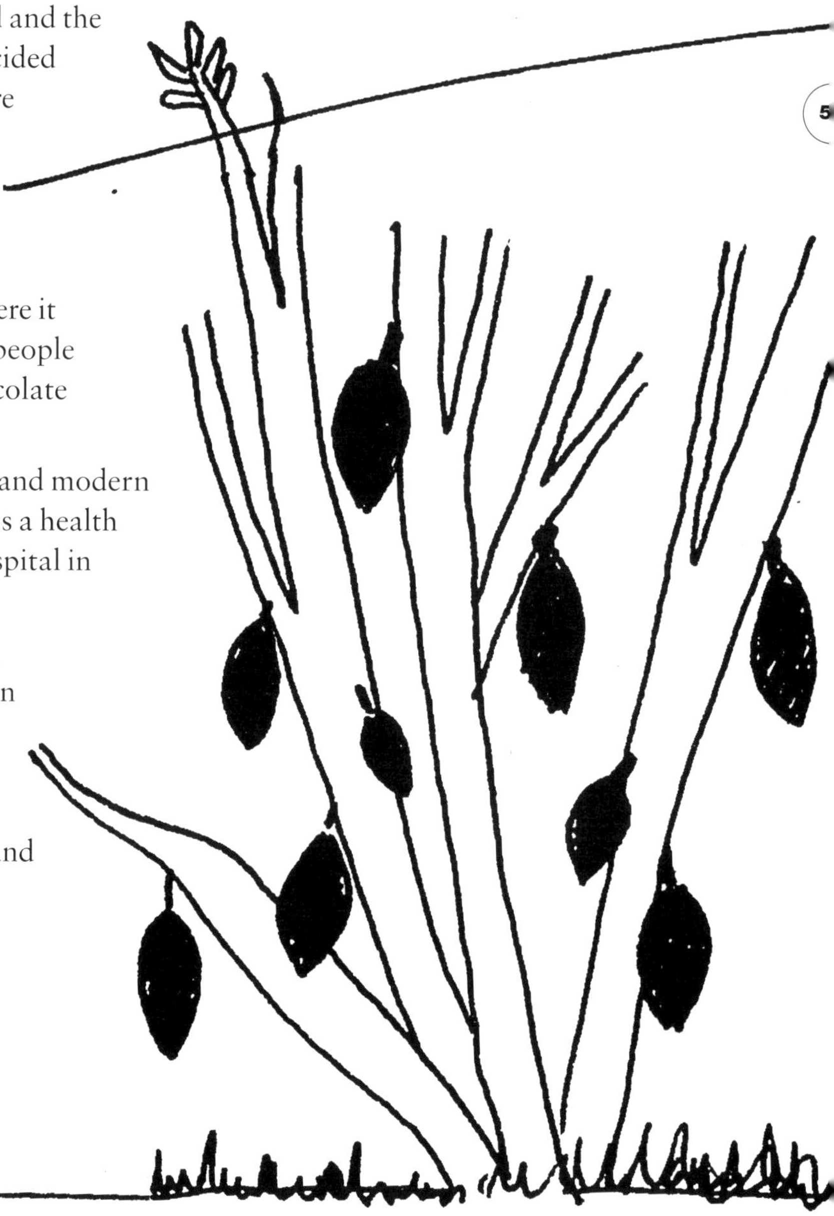

# Activity sheet 3 • Katonga Village in 1970 and 2000

## In 1970

## In 2000

**Key:** Wild animals, Herbs, Trees, Houses, Fish in the river, Rubbish in the river, Fields, Electricity, Health centre, Wild birds

## 1970

- There were five in total.
- There were many trees west of the river.
- People used herbs as medicines.
- No houses had electricity.
- It flowed in a south-easterly direction.
- Fish swam in the river.
- Birds nested in areas away from the houses.

## 2000

- It flows in a south-easterly direction.
- There are seven fields west of the river.
- Rubbish floats in the river.
- Most houses have electricity.
- There are 16 in total.
- There is a health centre near the bridge.
- They nest in areas away from the houses.

| Picture | | | | | | Picture |
|---|---|---|---|---|---|---|
| | In 1970 | | although<br>but | in 2000 | | |
| | In 1970 | | while<br>Today | in 2000 | | |
| | In 1970 | | A similarity is | in 2000 | | |
| | In 1970 | | However | in 2000 | | |
| | In 1970 | | It is the same because | in 2000 | | |
| | In 1970 | | whereas | in 2000 | | |

# Line drawings

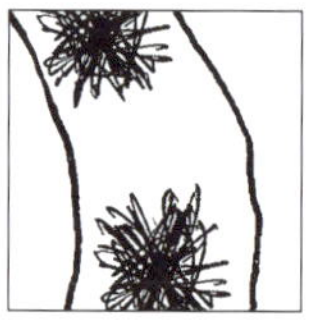

## Activity sheet 6 • Don't bin it – save it!

Many of the things in our rubbish bins can be recycled or used again. The average person in the UK throws out their own body weight in rubbish every three months.

T-shirts are made from cotton, which is a textile. Every year we throw away three quarters of a million tonnes of textiles. Old T-shirts can be donated to charity shops and jumble sales for other people to use. They can be put into rag banks and recycled into blankets and wiping cloths.

Many of the world's trees are cut down to make paper. Sketch pads are made from paper and these can be recycled in paper banks. It is good to use both sides of paper and use scrap paper for notes and messages. Opening envelopes carefully can save these too.

Water is often sold in glass bottles. These can be reused or taken to the bottle bank. There are 20,000 bottle banks in the UK.

Some chairs are made from wood. Old or broken chairs can be repaired or changed to look more modern. They can also be taken to second-hand furniture shops or charity shops and sold.

Batteries are made from heavy metals. They are small in size, but cause big pollution problems. It is better to buy cadmium-free batteries because they have fewer poisons. Also, rechargeable batteries can be used again and again.

Fruit peelings such as banana skins do not have to go in the rubbish bin. They can be put on a compost heap and after a few months can be used to improve the soil. In Austria, Denmark and Germany many people put fruit and vegetable waste in compost bins.

## Activity sheet 7 • Think before you bin it!

List everything you can see in the rubbish bin and use the information on activity sheet 6 to fill in the table below.

| Item | What is it made from? | How can it be recycled? |
|---|---|---|
| | | |
| | | |
| | | |
| | | |
| | | |
| | | |

## Activity sheet 8 • Are you environmentally friendly?

| Question | ✓or ✗ |
|---|---|
| Do you visit the recycling centre often? | |
| Do you ever plant a tree, some vegetables or flowers? | |
| Do you walk or cycle whenever you can, rather than go by car? | |
| Do you try to save water? | |
| Do you take showers instead of baths? | |
| Do you turn off the tap when you clean your teeth? | |
| Do you try to save electricity and gas? | |
| Do you turn off the TV when nobody is watching it? | |
| Do you use low energy light bulbs? | |

| Question | Answer |
|---|---|
| What rubbish is thrown away from your classroom? | |
| How much is thrown away in one week? | |
| How much of this waste can be recycled? ( 1/4, 1/2, 3/4 or all of it) | |
| Does your school recycle used paper, bottles and aluminium cans? | |

| How can you improve the situation in your school? | Put a number by each idea (1 is the best idea and 5 is the worst) |
|---|---|
| Have a recycling centre in school. | |
| Tell other classes about recycling. | |
| Have a rough paper tray. | |
| Tell the head teacher about recycling. | |
| Make posters about recycling. | |

## Activity sheet 9 • Being environmentally friendly

**There are many ways to be environmentally friendly.**

Before I began this topic I knew that ____________________________

______________________________________________________

When I read about it, I learnt some new things. For example, __________

______________________________________________________

I also learnt that ____________________________________

______________________________________________________

Another fact I learnt ____________________________________

We found out interesting facts about rubbish and recycling in school. For example, ______________________________________________

What surprised me most was ______________________________

______________________________________________________

However, the most surprising fact was ______________________

______________________________________________________

We have decided to improve our school by ____________________

______________________________________________________

Being environmentally friendly is important because ______________

______________________________________________________

| Mark | Meaning | Example |
|---|---|---|
|  | Delete words and sentences. | a very huge rubbish bin |
|  | Make the letter a capital. | In denmark |
|  | Make the letter lower case. | Use Both sides of paper. |
|  | Insert letters or words. | T-shirts are made from coton t |
|  | Make a space. | compostbins |
|  | Close a space. | furn iture |
|  | Move to a new place. | Scrap paper can be used for notes Use both sides of paper. |

# Unit three

## Persuasion

Year 5 term 3

**This unit will enable pupils to:**

- produce a piece of persuasive writing;
- understand how and why land rights trees are used;
- gain insight into life in Kukri Mukri, Bangladesh.

**In this unit you will find:**

- a two-week plan;
- a land rights tree;
- 12 photocopiable activity sheets;
- 4 colour photographs.

**Links to other curricular areas**

This unit also falls within the text range: year 4 term 3 (persuasion). It also relates to work covered in Key Stage 2 geography, English and citizenship education.

**Sonnai and Abul Hussain, Kukri Mukri, Bangladesh.**
PHOTO: LIBA TAYLOR

# Two-week plan

## Week one

### Day one text level 12

**Resources**

Photographs 9, 10, 11 and 12; activity sheet 1 (The Bangladesh Observer – stepped texts 1 to 4)

Read out and discuss activity sheet 1 – step 4 (OHT). Consider the newspaper report's intention to inform and gain attention.

Identify the issue, ie *Over half of the people on Kukri Mukri are landless*. Underline four of the problems in blue, eg *The land is really expensive*.

Pupils perform the above task, stepping through all four copies of the differentiated texts (these can be stapled together to form a booklet).

Read out and discuss the answers.

**Geography afternoon**

Look at photographs 9, 10, 11 and 12 of life in Kukri Mukri. Make a list of adjectives to describe the colours, shapes and textures in the photographs and use these to write detailed descriptions.

### Day two text level 12

**Resources**

Activity sheet 2 (A land rights tree); activity sheet 3 (A letter to the editor)

Look at the land rights tree (OHT) and generate questions. Read activity sheet 3 (OHT) and discuss the solutions.

Underline three of the solutions on activity sheet 3 (OHT), eg *Organise a protest march*. Label the problems and the solutions on the land rights tree.

Pupils perform the above task on their own.

Discuss which solution would be the most effective.

## **Day three** text level 15, sentence level 2

**Resources**

Activity sheet 4 (Persuading people – photocopy to A3); activity sheet 5 (Phrases used to persuade people)

Discuss the purpose of a poster persuading people to attend an event. Consider how the title catches people's attention and the use of short, snappy sentences.

Look at activity sheet 4 (OHT), choose an attention-seeking title, eg *March for the landless* and write down the time and place of the event. Write the sentences from the land rights tree in the appropriate boxes. Then look at activity sheet 5 (OHT) and add phrases to persuade people to the information in the boxes. See example.

**Example**

Not many people know that...
the land is really expensive

A shocking fact is...
many people can't read or sign the legal documents.

The time has come to take action.

Pupils perform the above task on their own.

Pupils orally develop sentences using information in the boxes, combining facts with phrases used to persuade people, eg *Everyone should know that landless people earn less than 30–40 taka (£1) a day.*



## **Day four** text level 18, sentence level 2, word level 3

**Resources**

Activity sheet 4

Read a pupil's example of activity sheet 4 (OHT). Consider how writing style and vocabulary are used to influence readers.

Write full sentences using information from each box and discuss which have the greatest impact in persuading people. These will form the basis of a poster.

Pupils design and write a poster, persuading people to attend the event, for 30 minutes, using IT. Include an attention-seeking title, information about where, when and why the event is taking place and phrases used to persuade people. Check spellings using the spell check and display.

**English afternoon**

Imagine the moon is going to be sold to a group of people. Read the list below and decide who you think should own the moon and why:

- rich people with the most money;
- people in the media who are good at advertising, eg selling moon rocks as souvenirs;
- people who are good at looking after their natural environment;
- people in the army who can defend the moon from attackers;
- people in education who can write books about what they find.

## **Day five** text levels 14 and 19

**Resources**

Activity sheet 6 (What makes a good poster?)

Read a pupil's example of a poster (OHT) and discuss its design and writing style.

Use activity sheet 6 (OHT) to evaluate the poster's impact in terms of persuasiveness and clarity of information. Make notes of the answers.

Pupils perform the above task in groups.

Groups present their conclusions to the class.

# Week two

## Day six

**Resources**

Activity sheet 7 (A problem solving tree – photocopy to A3); activity sheet 8 (Is it a problem or a solution?)

Look at activity sheet 7 (OHT) and generate questions. Brainstorm problems caused by bullying and solutions to the problems.

Read activity sheet 8 (OHT). Label the statements in the appropriate boxes on activity sheet 7, eg *Children do not want to go to school* goes in a *Problems caused by bullying* box.

Pupils perform the above task in pairs.

Read out and discuss the answers.

## **Day seven** text level 16

**Resources**

Activity sheet 7; activity sheet 9 (Bullying – problems and solutions)

Look at a pupil's example of activity sheet 7 (OHT) and discuss ideas about bullying. Make a list of these.

Choose the six strongest points from the pupils' ideas and the information on activity sheet 7. Write these in note form in the protest boxes on activity sheet 9 (OHT).

Pupils perform the above task on their own.

Read out and discuss activity sheet 9.

## **Day eight** text level 18, sentence level 2, word level 3

**Resources**

Activity sheet 9; activity sheet 10 (Writing a speech about bullying)

Look at activity sheet 10 (OHT) and consider how arguments are structured. Focus on the use of an opening statement, some of the problems associated with the argument, and solutions to these problems, and a summary statement.

Use the information on activity sheet 9 (OHT) to complete activity sheet 10 (OHT). This forms the basis of a speech about bullying. Pupils may choose to add extra detail and to structure their own writing.

Pupils write a speech arguing that there are problems caused by bullying and there are solutions to these problems, for 30 minutes, using IT. Check spellings using the spell check and present the speech to the class or at an assembly.

## **Day nine** text levels 16 and 18

**Resources**

Activity sheet 11 (No one deserves to be bullied)

Read out and discuss activity sheet 11 (OHT).

Underline the five most interesting facts about bullying. Underline the three most effective things your school can do to help people being bullied. Write these in note form in two numbered lists.



Pupils perform the above task on their own.

Read out and discuss answers.

## **Day ten** text level 17, sentence level 2, word level 1

**Resources**

Activity sheet 11; activity sheet 12 (Writing a petition)

Look at activity sheet 12 (OHT) and consider the purpose of petitions. Petitions:are aimed at people with the power to change situations; are based on a problem; provide information about the problem; suggest ways of improving the situation and encourage others to support the suggestions by writing their signatures.

Discuss who the petition is aimed at, eg *head teacher* and what the problem is about, eg *bullying in school*. Use activity sheet 11 (OHT) to fill in the remainder of activity sheet 12 (OHT). In the section asking for ways your school could help people being bullied, pupils could include what their school is already doing, eg *We would like our school to continue using the bully box*. Choose a title, eg *Three ways to stop bullying*.

Pupils write a petition for 30 minutes, by either filling in activity sheet 12 or using it as a template. Check spellings, collect signatures and use it.

BANGLADESH OBSERVER

30 July 2000 Price: 9 *taka*

# Whose land?

PHOTO: LIBA TAYLOR

Today's report comes from Kukri Mukri. Kukri Mukri is an island in Bangladesh. Sebila Yasmin lives on Kukri Mukri, and, like over half the islanders, she has no land.

Sebila told us why she has no land. "The land costs a lot of money," she said. "I have to borrow land from a rich landowner. Then I give him most of the crops I grow for free." She went on to say, "I also can't buy any land because I can't read or write. So I can't read and sign the forms needed to buy land."

Ranjit Khatan, a farmer, said, "I don't own any land and I have to work for a landowner. I earn less than £1 a day."

Sebila told us that the landowners fine people when they can't give them crops. Ranjit told us about a friend of his, who was fined when her crops were flooded.

BANGLADESH OBSERVER

30 July 2000 Price: 9 *taka*

# Whose land?

PHOTO: LIBA TAYLOR

Today's report comes from Kukri Mukri. Kukri Mukri is a small island in the south of Bangladesh. Sebila Yasmin lives on the island of Kukri Mukri, and, like over half the islanders, she has no land.

Sebila explained to us why she has no land. "The land costs a lot of money," she said. "I just can't afford the high prices so I have to borrow land from a rich landowner. Then I give him most of the crops I grow for free." She went on to say, "I also can't buy any land because I can't read or write. So I can't read and sign the forms needed for buying land."

Sebila's neighbour, Ranjit Khatan, said, "I don't own any land and I have to work long hours for a landowner. I earn less than 30–40 *taka* (£1) a day."

Sebila told us that the landowners fine people when they can't give them crops. Ranjit told us about a friend of his, who was fined when her crops were flooded. He said, "At times like these the last thing you need is a fine."

BANGLADESH OBSERVER

30 July 2000 Price: 9 *taka*

# Whose land?

PHOTO: LIBA TAYLOR

Today's report comes from the small island of Kukri Mukri. Kukri Mukri is in the Bay of Bengal in southern Bangladesh. Sebila Yasmin lives on Kukri Mukri, and, like over half of the islanders, she is landless.

Sebila explained to us why she owns no land. "The land here is expensive," she said. "I just can't afford the high prices and have to borrow land from the rich land-owner. Then I give him most of the crops I grow in return." She went on to say, "I also can't buy any land because I can't read or write. So I can't sign the documents needed to buy land in the first place."

Sebila's neighbour, Ranjit Khatan, said, "I am landless and I have to work for a landowner from dawn to dusk. I earn less than 30–40 *taka* (£1) a day, which is difficult to live on."

Another problem for landless people is borrowing money. Many are forced to borrow money from landowners and have to pay back more money. Sebila borrowed 2,000 *taka* to buy potato seeds and had to repay the landowner with 12 mounds of rice worth 3,000 *taka*.

Sebila revealed to us that when landless people can't repay the loans the landowners fine them. "When my friend's crops were destroyed by flooding, she was fined by the landowner," Ranjit told us. "At times like these the last thing you need is a heavy fine."

# BANGLADESH OBSERVER

30 July 2000 Price: 9 *Taka*

# Whose land?

Today's report comes from the small island of Kukri Mukri in the Bay of Bengal, southern Bangladesh. Sebila Yasmin, a mother of four, lives there, and, like over half of the islanders, she is landless.

PHOTO: LIBA TAYLOR

Sebila explained to us why she owns no land. "The land here is really expensive," she said. "I just can't afford the high prices. I have to pay a wealthy landowner to grow crops on his land. In return I give him most of my harvest and am left with hardly anything for my family." She continued, "Even if I had enough money I couldn't buy any land because I can't read or write. So I can't sign the legal documents needed to buy land in the first place. I feel really trapped."

Many landless people work long hours for the landowners. Sebila's neighbour, Ranjit Khatan, described the situation: "I am landless and I have to work for a landowner from dawn to dusk growing rice, beans, tea, potatoes and peppers. Landless people earn less than 30–40 *taka* (£1) a day, which is barely enough to live on."

Another problem facing landless people is borrowing money. Many are forced to borrow from landowners, who then demand repayment with high interest.

Sebila borrowed 2,000 *taka* to buy potato seeds and had to repay the landowner with 12 mounds of rice worth 3,000 *taka*. "This makes me really angry," she said, "because it makes it even more difficult to save enough money to buy land."

Sebila revealed to us that when landless people can't repay the loans the landowners fine them. Both Sebila and Ranjit know people who have been fined by landowners in the past year. "When my friend's crops were destroyed by flooding, she not only lost the harvest but was fined by the landlord," Ranjit told us. "At times like these the last thing you need is a heavy fine. People's lives are stressful enough as it is."

## Activity sheet 2 • A land rights tree

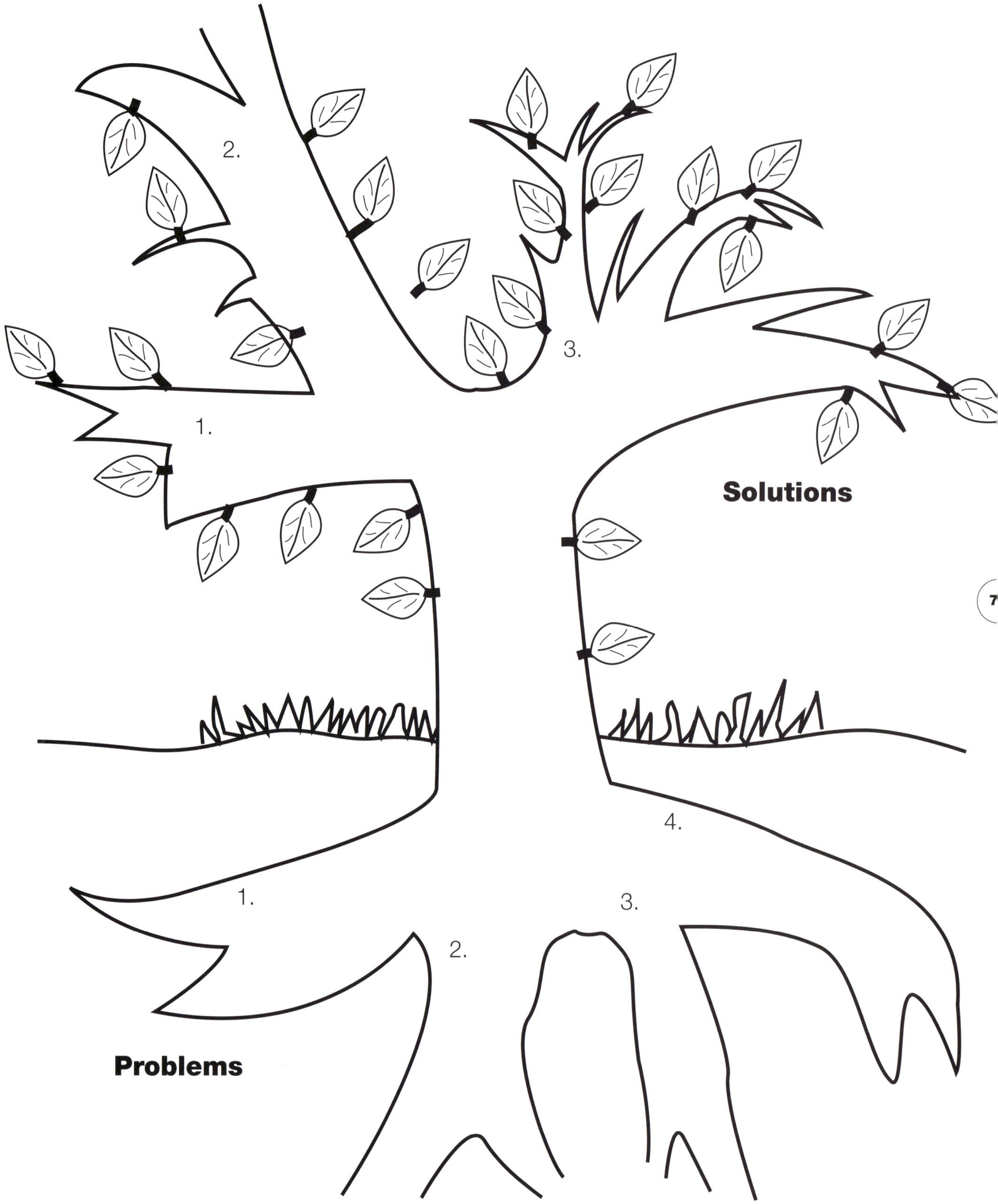


Issue: over half of the people on Kukri Mukri are landless.

# Activity sheet 3 • A letter to the editor

**1 September 2000**

Dear Editor,

We were interested to read one of the articles your newspaper published on 30 July. We are landless people living on the island of Kukri Mukri and discussed the land problem in our Reflect circle. This is what we came up with, and we would like you to publicise our letter in your newspaper.

We are pleased that you wrote an article about the land problem in Kukri Mukri because now lots of readers will learn about how difficult our lives can be. However, the negative tone of the article saddened us. Of course there are always problems, but we are also taking steps to improve the situation.

For example, in the Reflect circle we are learning to read and write. This is so we can read and sign the legal documents needed to buy land. We also employ local lawyers to check the documents.

Two months ago we decided to make a map of Kukri Mukri. We drew this on the ground first using sticks and stones to show how much of Kukri Mukri the landowners own. Then we copied it onto paper. The map showed that 80 per cent of Kukri Mukri is owned by landowners.

We are also going to organise a protest march on 7 October 2000. It will take place in the main bazaar on Kukri Mukri at 2.30pm. We are planning to march through the streets with banners telling people about the land problem. We realise we have strength when we act together.

Yours in solidarity

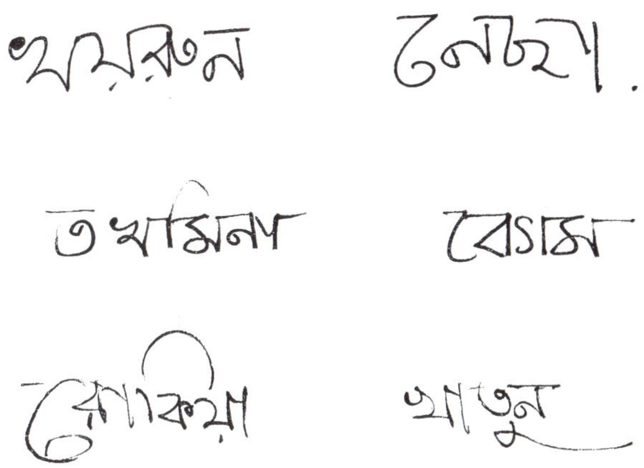

Signed by the members of a Kukri Mukri Reflect circle.

PS We are also sending a copy of this letter to the local and national governments.

# Activity sheet 4 • Persuading people

What event are you organising?
Think of a title to persuade people to attend.

Where is the event? (place)
When will the event take place? (date and time of day)

Picture

Why are you organising the event? Write down the issue.

Background information. Write down the problems.

# Activity sheet 5 • Phrases used to persuade people

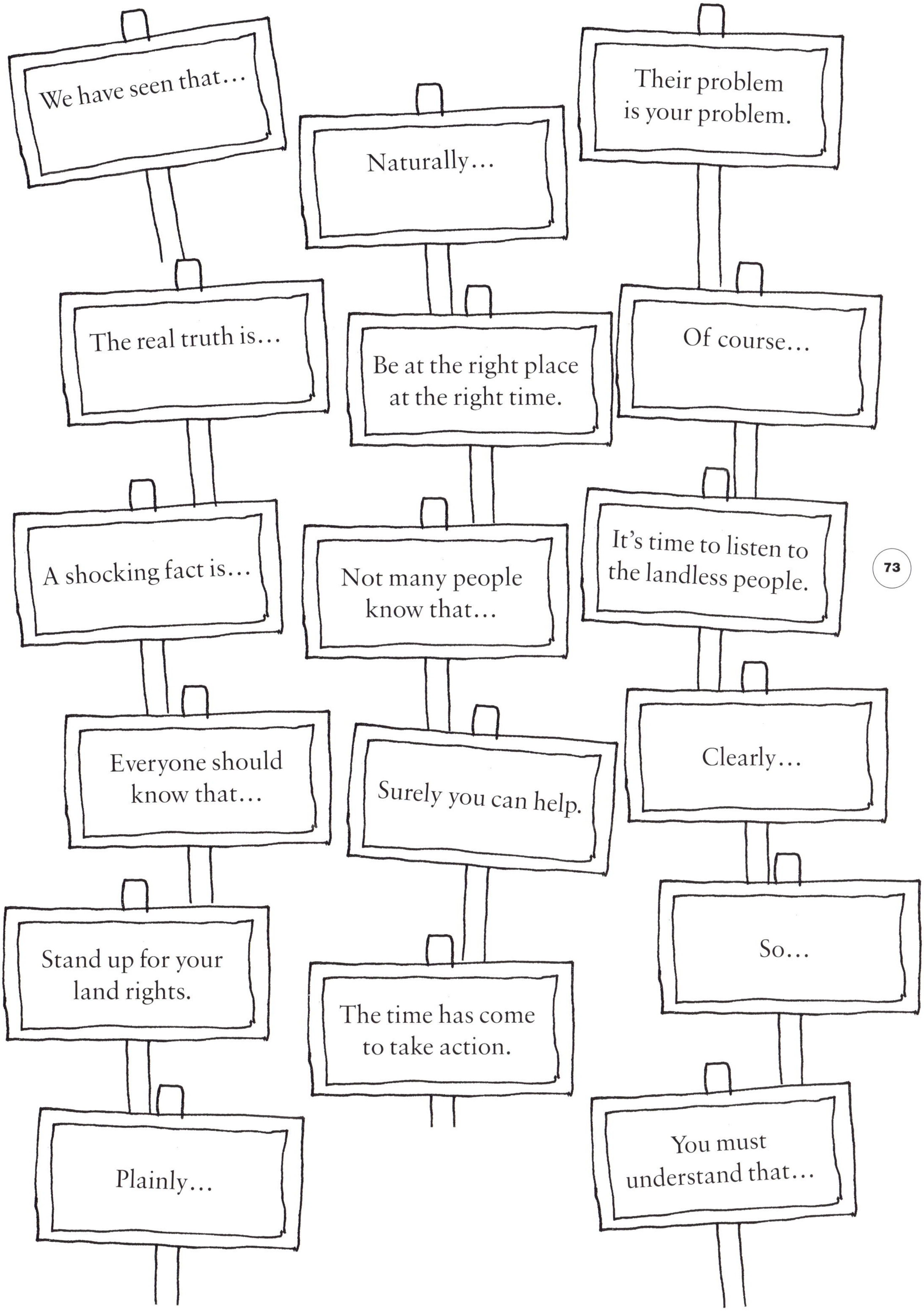

# Activity sheet 8 • Is it a problem or a solution?

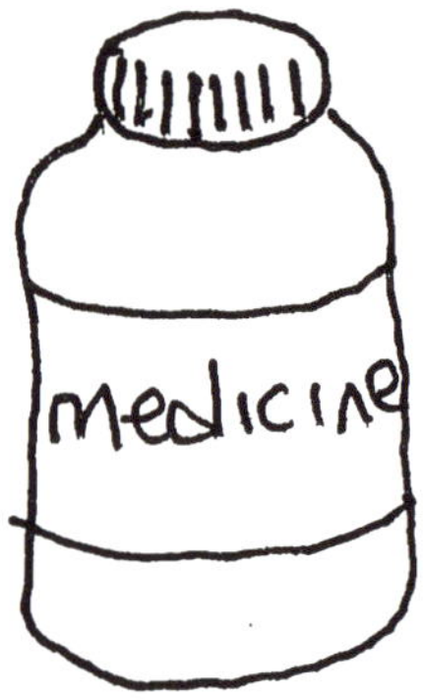


- Ignore the bully or say "No" very firmly. Then turn and walk away. It is hard for a bully to go on bullying someone who won't stand still to listen.
- People who are bullied find it hard to concentrate and their schoolwork gets worse.
- Children do not want to go to school. Some children pretend to feel ill in the mornings.
- People do not want to talk about what is wrong. They are quiet about how they feel.

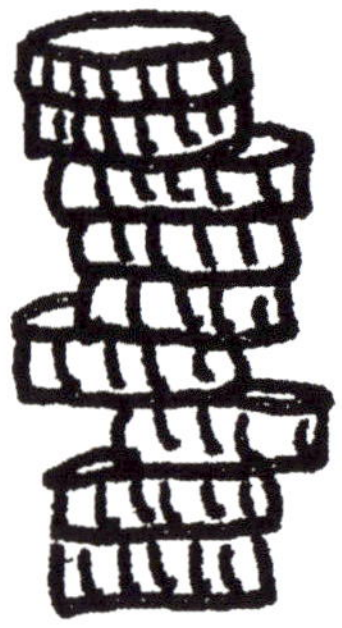

- Try not to be alone in places where you know the bully is likely to pick on you. This might put the bully off.
- Tell a friend or an adult about what is happening. Ask them to help you. You should not be silent if someone is hurting your feelings.
- People sometimes cry themselves to sleep and have nightmares about the bully.
- Try not to show that you are upset or angry. If you keep calm and hide how you feel, the bully might get bored and leave you alone.

- Children have less pocket money because the bully has taken it.
- Keep a diary of what is happening. Write down what has happened and how you feel. Then show someone.

## Activity sheet 8 • Is it a problem or a solution?

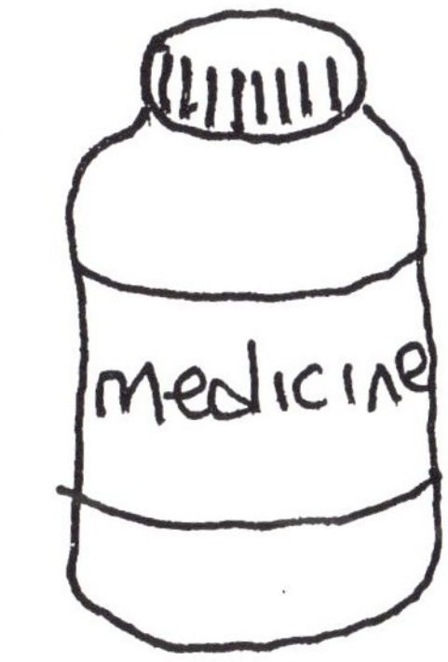


- Ignore the bully or say "No" very firmly. Then turn and walk away. It is hard for a bully to go on bullying someone who won't stand still to listen.
- People who are bullied find it hard to concentrate and their schoolwork gets worse.
- Children do not want to go to school. Some children pretend to feel ill in the mornings.
- People do not want to talk about what is wrong. They are quiet about how they feel.

- Try not to be alone in places where you know the bully is likely to pick on you. This might put the bully off.
- Tell a friend or an adult about what is happening. Ask them to help you. You should not be silent if someone is hurting your feelings.
- People sometimes cry themselves to sleep and have nightmares about the bully.
- Try not to show that you are upset or angry. If you keep calm and hide how you feel, the bully might get bored and leave you alone.

- Children have less pocket money because the bully has taken it.
- Keep a diary of what is happening. Write down what has happened and how you feel. Then show someone.

## Solutions to the problems

## Problems caused by bullying

- ...ink people will stop and read your poster when they ... title? Why?
- ...o you think the design of your poster is good? Why?
- What are the three most powerful things your poster says?
- Why is it important to have short and clear sentences on posters?
- Many posters try to be different and complicated to understand. Why is it important to keep the messages simple?

- Why have you included a picture?
- How well do you think it helps the writing?
- Is it better to have a picture with or without people in it? Why?

- How might the landless people feel about the poster?
- How might the landowners feel about the poster?
- How might the government feel about the poster?
- Would this poster persuade you to attend the event? Why?
- Would you like to improve your poster? How?

# Activity sheet 5 • Phrases used to persu

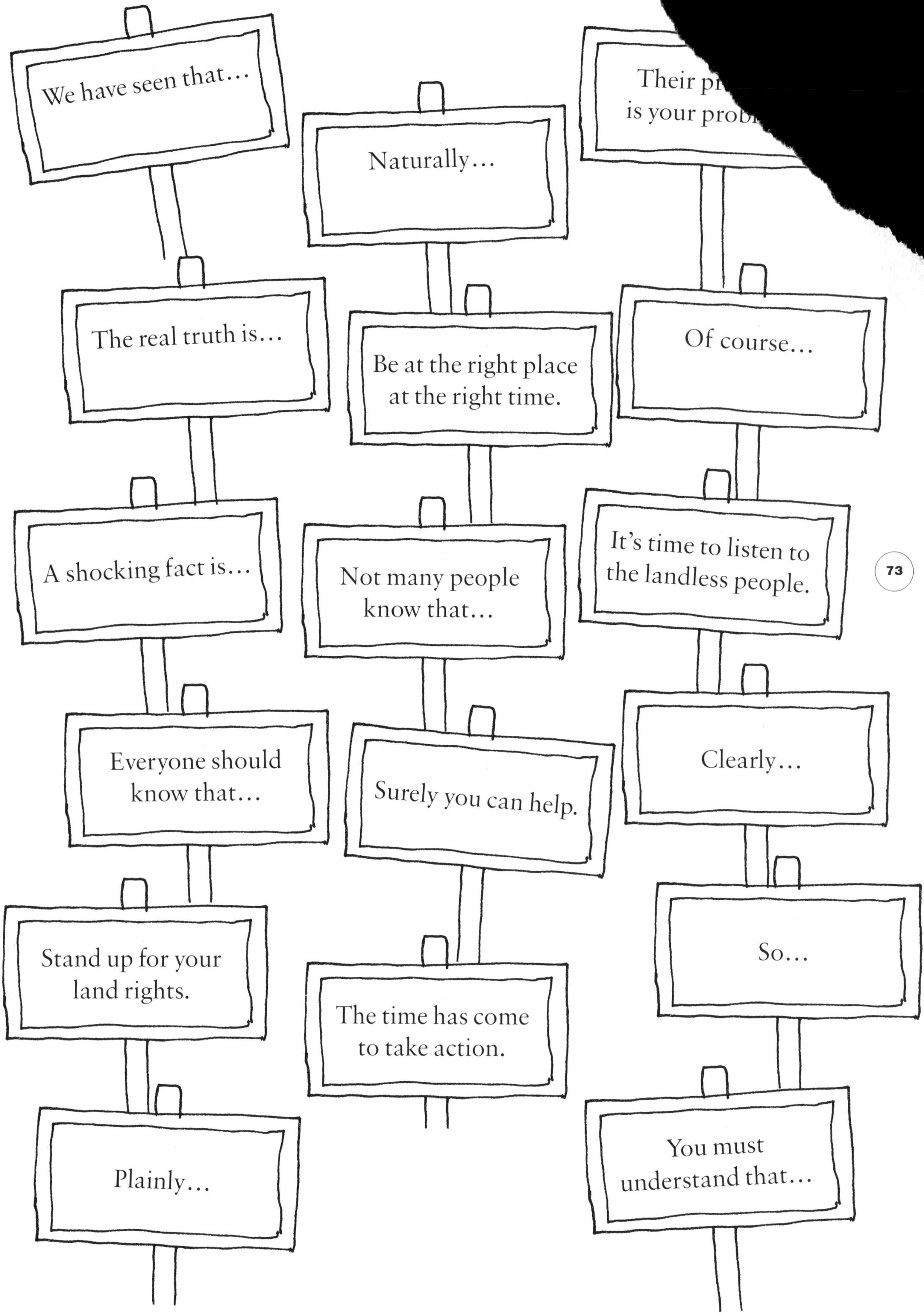

## Activity sheet 9 • Bullying – problems and solutions

**Argument:**
There are problems caused by bullying and there are solutions to these problems.

Write notes in the protest boxes to support this argument.

Protest box

| **Problem** | **Solution** |
| --- | --- |
| **Problem** | **Solution** |
| **Problem** | **Solution** |

# Activity sheet 10 • Writing a speech about bullying

I think ____________________________________________

____________________________________________________

There are many problems associated with bullying. One problem is ______

____________________________________________________

A second problem is ______________________________

____________________________________________

____________________________________________

Another problem is ______________________________________

____________________________________________________

____________________________________________________

However, there are solutions to some of these problems. One solution is

________________________________________

________________________________________

Also ____________________________________________

____________________________________________________

What's more ______________________________________

____________________________________________

Therefore, I think I have shown that ____________________

____________________________________________________

# Activity sheet 11 • No one deserves to be bullied

Anyone can be a target for the bully. Nearly everyone is bullied at some time in their lives. They can be bullied by brothers and sisters, by neighbours, by adults or by children. One expert says 1.3 million children a year are involved in bullying. Bullying can include name-calling, spreading rumours, teasing, pushing, kicking, hitting and pinching.

All schools have ways of dealing with bullying. Some schools have bully boxes, where children can leave notes about what is happening. Many schools have meetings or even councils where bullying is talked about. Here people work together to try and stop it.

Some schools have pupils or teachers for people to go to for help if they are being bullied. Other schools have posters on the walls, which tell people what to do if they are being bullied. All schools are very strict with bullies, but they also realise that bullies are often unhappy themselves and are trying to dump all their unhappiness on other people.

All sorts of people who are now successful adults were bullied when they were young. Tom Cruise, Geri Halliwell and Frank Bruno were all bullied when they were at school. They feel that bullying is wrong and that it was not their fault, but the fault of the bully looking for someone to hurt.

## Activity sheet 12 • Writing a petition

Title ____________________

This petition is aimed at ____________________

The problem is about ____________________

Here are five facts about the problem:

1. ____________________
2. ____________________
3. ____________________
4. ____________________
5. ____________________

We would like our school to:

1. ____________________
2. ____________________
3. ____________________

Sign below if you agree with this.

| | | |
|---|---|---|
| 1. ________ | 2. ________ | 3. ________ |
| 4. ________ | 5. ________ | 6. ________ |
| 7. ________ | 8. ________ | 9. ________ |
| 10. ________ | 11. ________ | 12. ________ |
| 13. ________ | 14. ________ | 15. ________ |
| 16. ________ | 17. ________ | 18. ________ |

# Recount

## Year 6 term 1

### This unit will enable pupils to:

- produce a piece of recount writing;
- understand how and why 24-hour recall circles are used;
- gain insight into life in Netrakona District, Bangladesh.

### In this unit you will find:

- a two-week plan;
- a 24-hour recall circle;
- 10 photocopiable activity sheets;
- 4 colour photographs.

**Links to other curricular areas**

This unit also falls within the text range: year 5 term 1 (recount); year 5 term 2; year 6 term 1 and year 6 term 3 (non-chronological report). It also relates to work covered in Key Stage 2 geography, English and citizenship education.

**Pupils from Leominster Junior school, Herefordshire, UK.**
PHOTO: HELEN MEREDITH

# Two-week plan

## Week one

### Day one text level 11

**Resources**

Photographs 13, 14, 15 and 16; 24-hour recall circle; activity sheet 1 (Tasmil's day); activity sheet 2 (Hasima's day)

Look at photographs 13, 14, 15 and 16 and the 24-hour recall circle (OHT) and generate questions, eg what does the grey semicircle represent? (night)

Read out and discuss activity sheet 1 (OHT). Consider how recounts are often written in the first person and the past tense. Use the 24-hour recall circle (OHT) and activity sheet 1 (OHT) to complete activity sheet 2 (OHT). See example.

**Example**

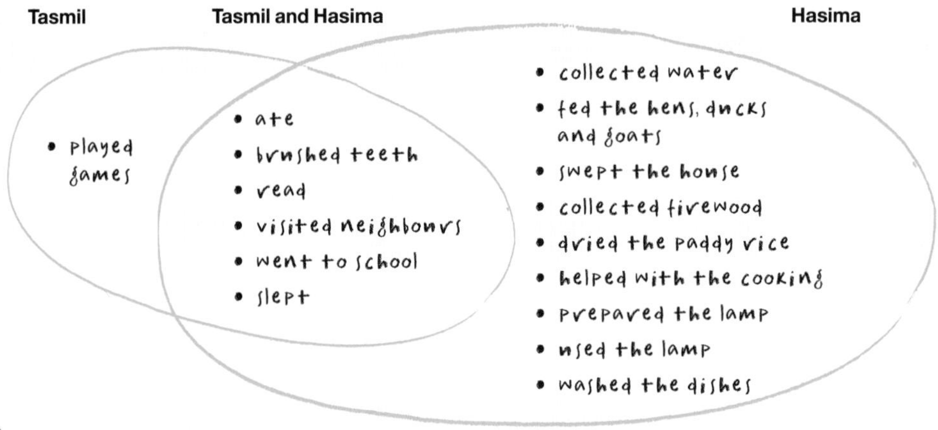


Pupils perform the above task in pairs.

Read out answers and relate them to the 24-hour recall circle.

**Geography afternoon**

Pupils create their own 24-hour recall circles in pairs of one boy and one girl. Compare it with Tasmil and Hasima's versions.

### Day two text level 14

**Resources**

24-hour recall circle; activity sheet 1; activity sheet 2; activity sheet 3 (The beginning of Hasima's letter)

Read out and discuss the first two paragraphs of activity sheet 1 (OHT).

Use activity sheet 1 (OHT) and activity sheet 2 (OHT) to complete activity sheet 3 (OHT). This forms the beginning of Hasima's letter, which the pupils are going to produce by the end of the week. Write in the role of Hasima in the first person and the past tense, eg *I filled in the 24-hour recall circle on 23 February with a friend called Tasmil. We completed it in a geography lesson in school.*

Pupils perform the above task on their own.

Pupils present the beginning of Hasima's letter to the class, relating it to the 24-hour recall circle.

## Day three text level 14

**Resources**

24-hour recall circle; activity sheet 1; activity sheet 4 (The middle of Hasima's letter – photocopy to A3)

Read out and discuss paragraphs 3 to 7 on activity sheet 1 (OHT). Focus on the use of temporal connectives and chronological sequencing in recount writing.

Use the 24-hour recall circle (OHT) and activity sheet 1 (OHT) to complete activity sheet 4 (OHT). Write full sentences in the role of Hasima and add detail, eg *Between 1800 and 2100 I used the lamp because it was getting dark. Then I helped my mother with the cooking and eventually ate some food.*

Pupils perform the above task on their own.

Pupils present the beginning and middle part of Hasima's letter to the class, relating it to the 24-hour recall circle.

## Day four text levels 11 and 14

**Resources**

Activity sheet 1; activity sheet 5 (The end of Hasima's letter)

Read out and discuss paragraph 8 of activity sheet 1 (OHT). Consider the differences between facts and opinions. Show how the beginning and middle of Tasmil's letter are factual and the end is based on opinion.

Read out and complete activity sheet 5 (OHT). Tick whether each quote is a fact or an opinion and give reasons for this, eg The quote is an opinion because it says what Hasima thinks and feels about the 24-hour recall circle. Write the three opinions in your own words to form the end of Hasima's letter.

Pupils perform the above task in pairs, each completing their own activity sheet 5.

Volunteers read out the concluding paragraph of Hasima's letter and answer pupils' questions (hot seating).

## Day five text levels 14 and 18

**Resources**

Activity sheet 1; pupil's activity sheets 3, 4 and 5

Look at activity sheet 1 and consider the layout of letters.

Read pupils' examples of activity sheets 3, 4 and 5 and revise the main features of recount writing.

Pupils write a detailed recount, in the form of a letter from Hasima for 30 minutes, using IT. Write in chronological order using the first person and the past tense and include facts and opinions. Check spellings using the spell check and display with the 24-hour recall circle and Tasmil's letter.

# Week two

## Day six text levels 11 and 13

**Resources**

Activity sheet 6 (Mubarakpur Primary School newsletter)

Read activity sheet 6. Focus on the formal writing style of non-chronological reports and compare this with recount writing, eg distinguish between the use of the third and first person.

Underline the four action points in the text. Make a list of these and write them into the first person, eg *The girls and boys would swap jobs for one day* could become *We decided to swap jobs for one day* and *Make sure the girls have free time to play games and enjoy themselves* could become *We wanted the girls to have free time to play games* and enjoy themselves.

Pupils perform the above activity in pairs.

Read out and discuss the action points.

## Day seven text level 14

**Resources**

Pupils' action points; 24-hour recall circle; activity sheet 6; activity sheet 7 (Live on Radio Netrakona!)



Read the pupils' action points and activity sheet 7. Focus on the use of speech punctuation.

Use the pupil's action points, the 24-hour recall circle and activity sheet 6 to complete activity sheet 7 in the role of one of the children.

Pupils perform the above task on their own.

Pupils role-play the interviews in pairs. This could be taped and played back during an assembly.

**English afternoon**

Design a poster of the interview using speech bubbles.

## Day eight

**Resources**

Activity sheet 8 (Survey sheet)

Ask the pupils to close their eyes and imagine an international football player scoring a goal. Then ask them to sketch what they saw. How many pupils saw a female football player?

Read out and discuss activity sheet 8 (OHT). Put ticks or numbers in the appropriate boxes.

Pupils perform the above task in mixed sex groups.

Discuss the answers. Is there a difference between the girls' and boys' responses?

## Day nine text level 11

**Resources**

Activity sheet 8; activity sheet 9 (Girls' football – more than a game!)

Read out and discuss activity sheet 9 (OHT). Revise the features of recount writing.

Underline the problem in red, ie *girls weren't allowed to join the club because football was seen to be a boys' game*, and the solutions in blue, eg o*rganise girls' football matches*. Use activity sheet 8 to find problems associated with gender divisions and sport in your school, eg *boys using most of the playground for sport at breaktimes and girls not having as much exercise as boys*. Brainstorm possible solutions to the problem. See example.

**Example**

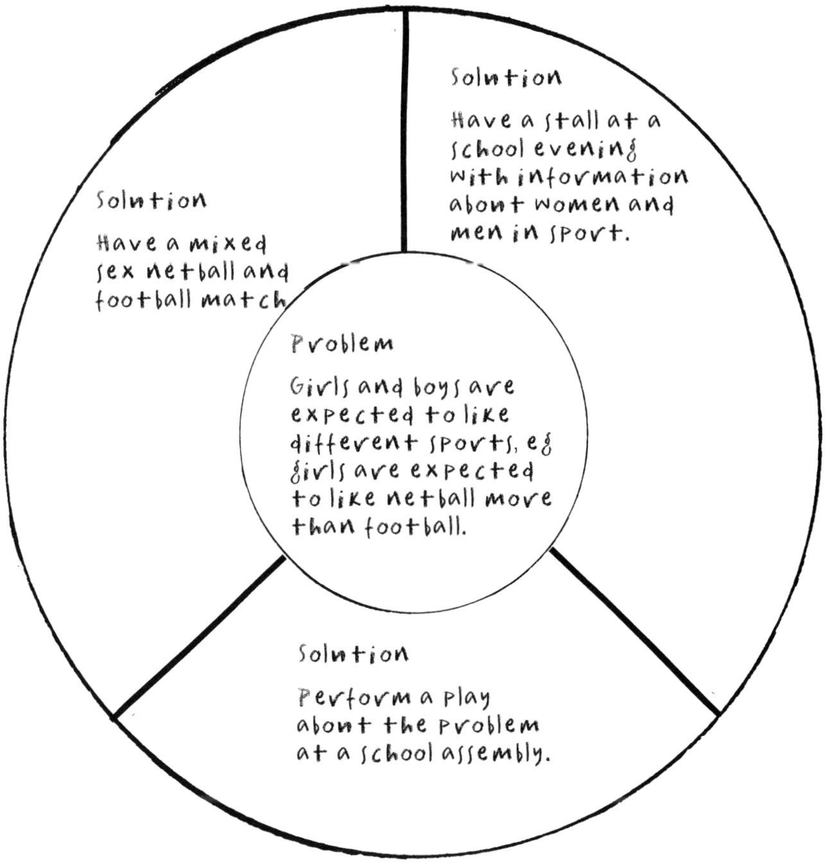


Pupils perform the above task in mixed sex groups.

Discuss which solution would raise the most publicity.

## Day ten text levels 15 and 18

**Resources**

Activity sheet 10 (Press release)

Look at activity sheet 10 (OHT) and consider the purpose and layout of press releases.

Choose one solution from day nine and complete activity sheet 10 (OHT).

Pupils write a press release for 30 minutes using activity sheet 10 as a template. Use IT to plan and edit the press release to bring it up to publication standard. Then use it.

# A 24-hour recall circle

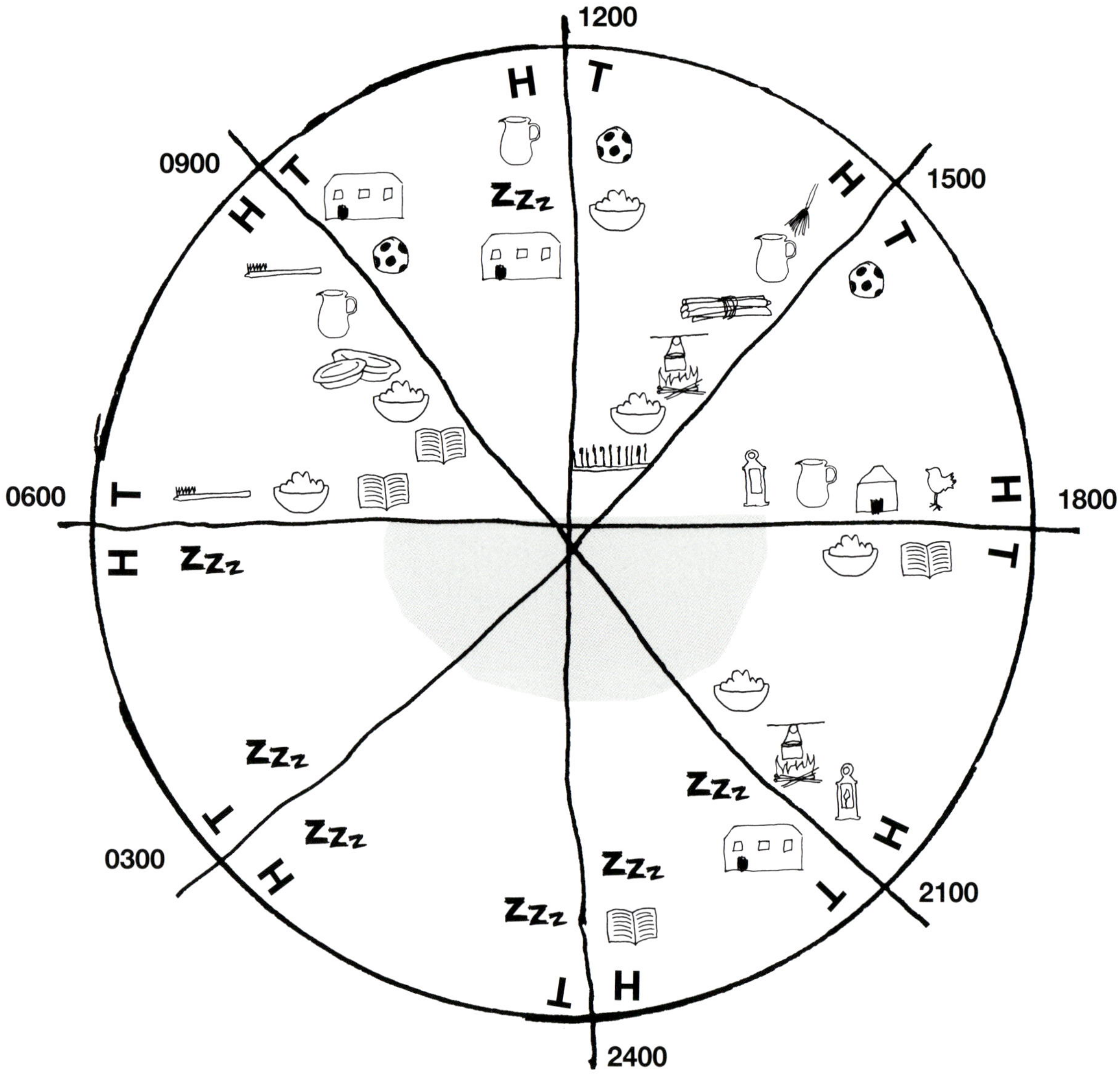


H Hasima

T Tasmil

ate

collected firewood

dried the paddy rice

prepared the lamp

Zzz slept

used the lamp

washed the dishes

brushed my teeth

collected water

played games

read

swept the house

visited neighbours

went to school

fed the hens, ducks and goats

helped with the cooking

## Activity sheet 1 • Tasmil's day

**Mubarakpur Village**
**Netrakona District**
**Bangladesh**

3 March 2000

Dear class,

Hello, my name is Tasmil and I am an 11-year-old boy. I'm from Mubarakpur Village in Netrakona District, which is located in the north-eastern corner of Bangladesh. It is a rural area, and wherever you look lush, green fields stretch far into the distance. It's a wonderful sight.

This letter tells you how I spent 23 February 2000. The 24-hour recall circle shows what I did every three hours. We filled it in at school and worked in pairs. A girl called Hasima was my partner. She is 11 years old and lives in Mubarakpur Village too.

Now I'd like to tell you about my day. Between 2400 and 0600 I was sleeping in my bed. At 0600 I woke up, cleaned my teeth, ate some breakfast and read a book. At 0900 I went to school. I studied many subjects including maths, geography and Bengali, the main language of Bangladesh. Hasima and I completed the 24-hour recall circle in our geography lesson.

After studying, I started playing *kabadi*, which is the national game of Bangladesh. *Kabadi* can last for hours and we were still playing it at 1200. It was a great game and I really enjoyed myself, especially because my team won.

Eventually we finished and I decided to get something to eat. I felt really hungry after playing *kabadi*, so I went home and ate some food.

Between 1500 and 1800 I played football and cricket. I was a striker in the football match and a wicket keeper in the cricket game. We lost the football, but we didn't finish the cricket match, because it was starting to get dark.

By 1800 I felt happy but exhausted. I went to my home, read some school books and ate a big meal. I had rice with garlic and chilli sauce, which is my favourite food. At 2100 I walked to a neighbour's house to see how they were and to tell them about the *kabadi*, football and cricket games. Finally I strolled home and went to bed. I needed to rest before another day of activities.

I hope you've enjoyed reading about my life. In my opinion, I have a good time playing all the games I love. I also think it must have been interesting for you to learn about how I spend an average day.

Best wishes, Tasmil

# Activity sheet 2 • Hasima's day

| |
|---|
| How old is Hasima? |
| What is the name of the village where Hasima lives? |
| What is the name of the district where Hasima lives? |
| What is the name of the country where Hasima lives? |
| List two facts about the area where Hasima lives.<br>1.<br>2. |

| |
|---|
| When did Hasima fill in the 24-hour recall circle? |
| Who did Hasima fill it in with? |
| Where did Hasima fill it in? |

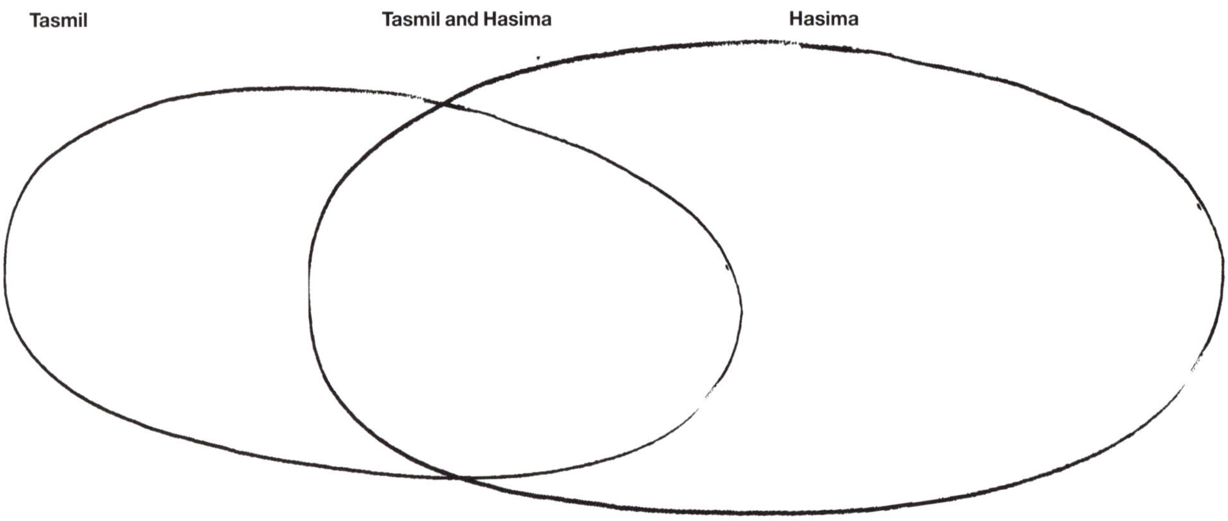




| |
|---|
| What activities did Tasmil and Hasima do? |
| How many activities did Tasmil do? |
| How many activities did Hasima do? |
| How many of the same activities did Tasmil and Hasima do? |
| Which of these activities are jobs? |

## Activity sheet 3 • The beginning of Hasima's letter

Address ______________________

______________________

Date ______________________

______________________

Dear class,

Introduce yourself and write information about where you live.

eg *My name is Hasima and I am* ________ *years old. I live…* ____________

______________________________________________

______________________________________________

______________________________________________

Write about the 24-hour recall circle.

eg *I filled in the 24-hour recall circle on* ______________________

______________________________________________

______________________________________________

______________________________________________

______________________________________________

Write about the number of jobs Hasima and Tasmil did.

eg *Throughout the day I did* ________ *jobs.*

______________________________________________

______________________________________________

______________________________________________

# Activity sheet 4 • The middle of Hasima's letter

| 2400 to 0600 |
|---|
| 0600 to 0900 |
| 0900 to 1200 |
| 1200 to 1500 |
| 1500 to 1800 |
| 1800 to 2100 |
| 2100 to 2400 |

Word bank

At _____

Then

In the morning

Next

Before _____

From _____ to _____

Following _____

During this time

Meanwhile

Afterwards

In the afternoon

Later

Between _____ and _____

Eventually

Finally

By _____

## Activity sheet 5 • The end of Hasima's letter

Read the four quotes by Hasima and decide if you think they are fact or opinion. Explain why you think this is.

**Quote**

"It doesn't seem fair that I have so much housework to do. I wish I had more time for schoolwork."

Fact? ☐ Opinion? ☐ because ______________________________

______________________________________________________

**Quote**

"I believe the boys spend too much time playing games and it makes me angry. I play games on the weekend, but would love to do it every day."

Fact? ☐ Opinion? ☐ because ______________________________

______________________________________________________



**Quote**

"Girls have to do far more work than boys. For example, when the boys play *kabadi*, football and cricket, we are helping our mothers in the house."

Fact? ☐ Opinion? ☐ because ______________________________

______________________________________________________

**Quote**

"I feel that filling in the 24-hour recall circle was really valuable, because it showed how much work the girls do. I think the boys were surprised and may talk about how to make things better."

Fact? ☐ Opinion? ☐ because ______________________________

______________________________________________________

Write a paragraph about Hasima's opinions to end the letter.

______________________________________________________

______________________________________________________

______________________________________________________

# MUBARAKPUR PRIMARY SCHOOL NEWSLETTER

PHOTO: ELAINE DUIGENAN

On 23 February 2000, children from class 7 (10–11 year-olds) made a 24-hour recall circle. They wanted to fill in the 24-hour recall circle in order to find out more about how they spend their days. The results were fascinating.

The 24-hour recall circle showed that the girls did far more work than the boys. The girls did not realise how much work they did and the boys were surprised about the amount of time they spend playing games. Both the girls and the boys decided to take action to improve the problem.

The children made a list of action points in their geography lessons. The first action point was that the girls and boys would swap jobs for one day. The girls would do what the boys normally do, and the boys would do what the girls normally do. They thought this would be a fun and entertaining way to look at the problem.

All over the world many people think that housework is easy and not very important. In Mubarakpur Village housework is done by the girls and the women, while the men work outside the home.

The children decided that this wasn't fair and they wrote down a second action point. The boys would help with the housework and share some of the jobs. They said they would sweep the house and help with the cooking. Then the girls and the boys would understand each other's lives better and the girls would have more time for other things. The third action point was to make sure the girls have free time to play games and enjoy themselves.

At the moment the boys spend much more time in school than girls. This is because many people in the area think boys need more education than girls, so they can get paid jobs and earn money in the future. The children thought the girls should also have this opportunity and their final action point was to persuade their parents to send their daughters to school.

Mubarakpur Primary School is very proud of the children for making the 24-hour recall circle and thinking of so many action points. We hope that whoever reads this newsletter will look at a problem and take action to make their situation better.

## Activity sheet 7 • Live on Radio Netrakona!

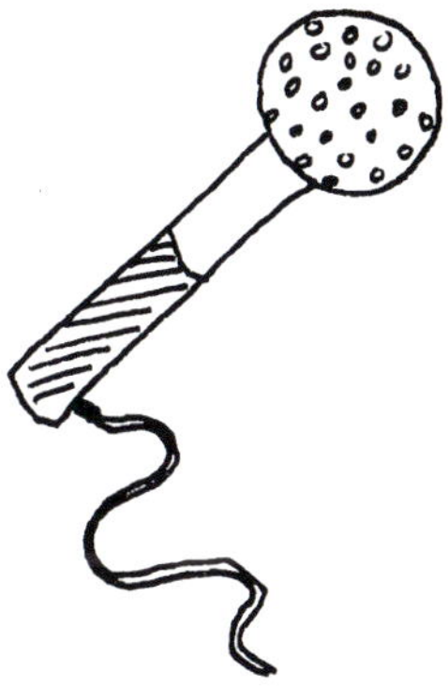

"Good morning listeners. Today we are reporting from Mubarakpur Village. We have travelled to the village to interview the children of Mubarakpur Primary School.

Now I've heard that you've done something really special in your geography lessons. Tell us what you did."

" ____________________________________________

____________________________________________ "

"This 24-hour recall circle sounds fabulous and I'm sure everyone wants to know one interesting fact about it. What can you tell us?"

" ____________________________________________

____________________________________________ "

"Now here's the best bit. I've heard you decided to take action to make things better. What was your first action point?"

" ____________________________________________ "

"What was your second action point?"

" ____________________________________________ "

"Was there a third action point?"

" ____________________________________________ "

"Are there any other action points?"

" ____________________________________________ "

"Four action points! Now that's incredible. Please tell us more about one of the action points and why you think it's important."

"Well, thanks very much for letting us interview you. I'm sure the listeners are really impressed with the work you've done. It's great when children do things to make us all think about our lives!"

# Activity sheet 8 • Survey sheet

## Boy's name

______________________________

Do you play sport at break time?

Yes ☐ No ☐ Sometimes ☐

Who do you play sport with at break time?

Boys ☐ Girls ☐ Both ☐

How much of the school playground do you take up playing sport?

A small part of it ☐

A large part of it ☐

Rank the reasons why you play sport. (1 = first reason; 4 = last reason)

It keeps you fit and healthy ☐

It is fun and exciting ☐

It is a part of PE lessons ☐

To be with your friends ☐

Rank the sports you play most often. (1 = most often, 10 = least often)

cricket ☐

rounders ☐

swimming ☐

netball ☐

athletics ☐

football ☐

rugby ☐

volleyball ☐

gymnastics ☐

hockey ☐

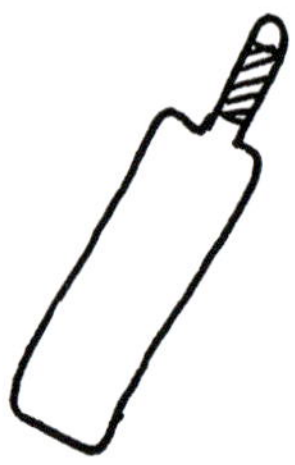

Look at numbers 9 and 10 on your list. Why don't you play these sports very often?

______________________________

## Girl's name

______________________________

Do you play sport at break time?

Yes ☐ No ☐ Sometimes ☐

Who do you play sport with at break time?

Boys ☐ Girls ☐ Both ☐

How much of the school playground do you take up playing sport?

A small part of it ☐

A large part of it ☐

Rank the reasons why you play sport. (1 = first reason; 4 = last reason)

It keeps you fit and healthy ☐

It is fun and exciting ☐

It is a part of PE lessons ☐

To be with your friends ☐

Rank the sports you play most often. (1 = most often, 10 = least often)

cricket ☐

rounders ☐

swimming ☐

netball ☐

athletics ☐

football ☐

rugby ☐

volleyball ☐

gymnastics ☐

hockey ☐

Look at numbers 9 and 10 on your list. Why don't you play these sports very often?

______________________________

## Activity sheet 9 • Girl's football – more than game!

Hi! My name is Sarah and I'm a member of the Mathare youth sports club in Nairobi, the capital city of Kenya. Kenya is a country in East Africa and I have lived here all my life. I joined the Mathare youth sports club when I was nine years old and today it is the largest youth football club in Africa. Our motto is 'Giving youth a sporting chance'.

I wanted to join the club when I was seven, but I couldn't because of a big problem. The problem was girls weren't allowed to join the club because football was seen as a boys' game. This upset me, as I love football.

I have many female friends who also love football, so we decided to find some solutions to the problem. Our first solution was to tell the Mathare youth sports club how we felt and that girls would like to be members.

PHOTO: GLEN WILLIAMS/STRATEGIES FOR HOPE

Our second solution was to organise girls' football matches. The boys laughed at the idea. Some of them felt football was a boys' game and girls were needed to work at home.

Eventually the Mathare youth sports club listened to us. Our third solution was to encourage them to set up a three-year programme to improve girls' football skills. To our surprise they agreed to do this.

Four experienced boys trained us and helped organise girls' football teams. After a short time we were playing in mixed teams with the boys and now I train some of the younger girls and boys. I was recently a defender in the quarter finals of the world's largest international youth football tournament.

Peter Sherry is the co-ordinator of the Mathare youth sports club and he told us, "Boys are coming to have more respect for the girls and the girls are becoming more self-confident."

# Activity sheet 10• Press release

Date ______________________________

Name of school ______________________________

Headline

[ ]

We are concerned about girls and boys in sport. A problem at our school is

[ ]

On the ________________ (date) we are going to try and solve the problem.
We are going to

[ ]

For more information please contact

Name ______________________________

Address ______________________________

______________________________

______________________________

Telephone number ______________________________

# Unit five

## Explanation

Year 6 term 3

**This unit will enable pupils to:**

- produce a piece of explanation writing linked to geography;
- understand how and why mobility maps are used;
- gain insight into life in Kukri Mukri, Bangladesh.

**In this unit you will find:**

- a two-week plan;
- a mobility map;
- 8 photocopiable activity sheets;
- 4 colour photographs;
- line drawings.

**Links to other curricular areas**

This unit also falls within the text range: year 4 term 3 (explanation); year 5 term 2 (explanation); year 5 term 1 (recount); year 6 term 1 (recount).

It also relates to work covered in Key Stage 2 geography and citizenship education.

Pupils from Mantorba Primary School, Bundibugyo, Uganda.

PHOTO: TAAHRA GHAZI

# Two-week plan

## Week one

### **Day one** text level 17

**Resources**

Mobility map; activity sheet 1 (Sonnai's recount – stepped texts 1 to 4)

Look at the mobility map (OHT) and generate questions. Match the nine nouns at the bottom of the map with the sketches. Study the scale and direction.

Read out and discuss activity sheet 1 – step 4 (OHT). Underline the nine nouns from the map in blue, eg *pond* and the past tense action verbs, relating to these nouns in red, eg *observed (wildlife)* and *captured (insects)*.

Pupils work through the above task, stepping through all four copies of the differentiated texts. These can be stapled together to form a booklet.

Discuss the use of verbs to describe actions.

**Geography afternoon**

Look at photographs 17, 18, 19 and 20 and match them with the places on Sonnai's mobility map.



### **Day two** text level 15

**Resources**

Mobility map; line drawings; activity sheet 1; activity sheet 2 (Mobility map outline); activity sheet 3 (Action verbs word bank). Photocopy activity sheet 2 to A3.

Introduce the four photographs and match them with the appropriate symbols on the mobility map (OHT).

Cut out the line drawings and put them next to the appropriate boxes on the mobility map outline (OHT). Add the underlined nouns and action verbs from activity sheet 1 to the appropriate boxes, eg *tube well* and *collected (water)* go in the *tube well* box. Add two present tense action verbs from activity sheet 3 in black to each box next to words with a similar meaning, eg *rush* goes with *hurried* in the *cyclone shelter* box. Discuss how recounts are written in the past tense and explanations are written in the present tense. Underline the present tense action verbs.

Pupils perform the above task on their own.

Read out and discuss the new action verbs.

## **Day three** text level 19

### Resources

Sonnai's recount; activity sheet 2; activity sheet 4 (Words to do with time)

Read activity sheet 1 – step 4 (OHT). Consider the similarities between recount and explanation writing, eg temporal connectives.

Look at activity sheet 4 (OHT) and brainstorm other temporal connectives. Add these to activity sheet 2 (OHT), eg *First* goes in the *animal pens* box and *In emergencies* goes in the *cyclone shelter* box. Choose a title for the mobility map, eg *Sonnai's mobility map*, and a subtitle for each box, eg *Learning at school*. See example.

### Example

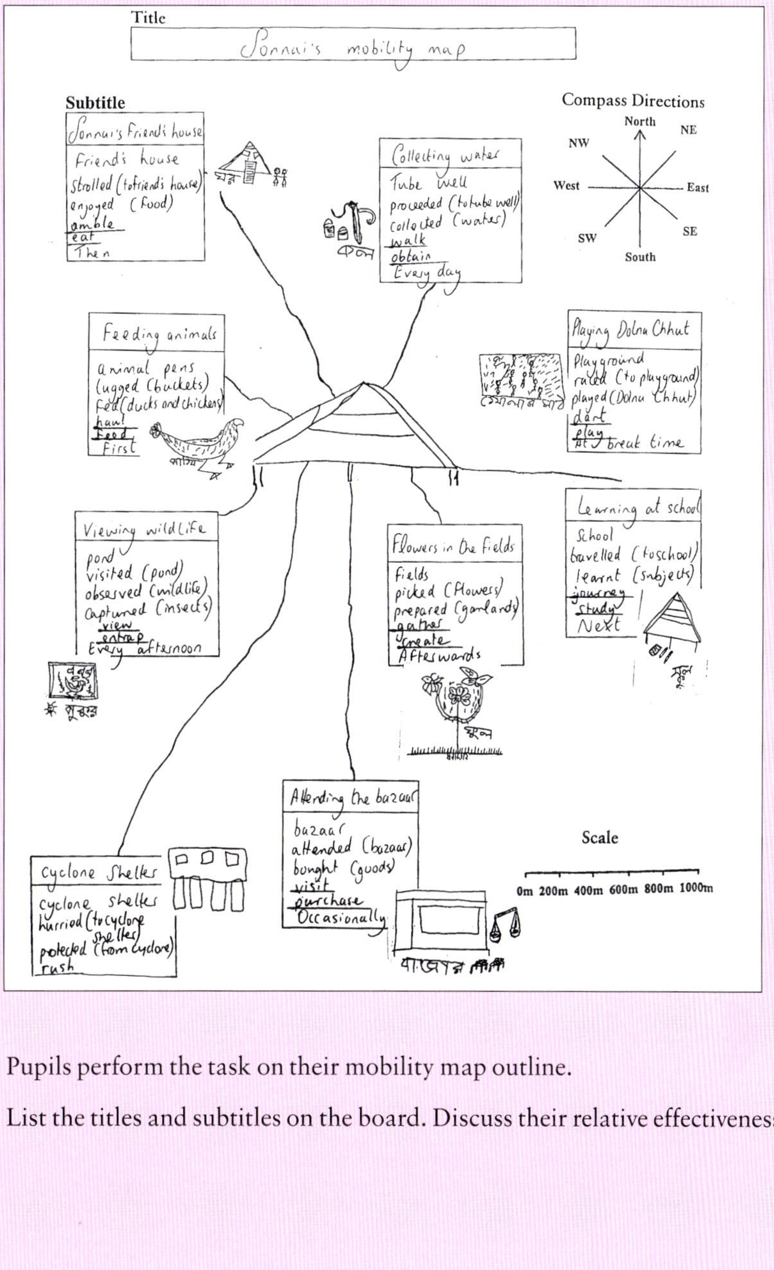


Pupils perform the task on their mobility map outline.

List the titles and subtitles on the board. Discuss their relative effectiveness.

## **Day four** text level 16

**Resources**

Sonnai's recount; activity sheet 2; activity sheet 5 (Building sentences – photocopy to A3 size)

Read activity sheet 1 – step 4 (OHT). Consider the differences between recount and explanation writing, eg the use of tenses. Focus on the present tense and formal style of explanation writing.

Look at a pupil's example of activity sheet 2 (OHT). Identify the temporal connectives and add these to the first section of activity sheet 5 (OHT). Identify the present tense action verbs and add these to the second and fourth sections of activity sheet 5. Verbs need to be in the plural form in the fourth section, eg *feed the chickens*. Develop full sentences, using the words and phrases from all four sections of activity sheet 5. There can be a range of combinations, eg *Sometimes Sonnai walks to the bazaar in order to choose some goods* and *Occasionally Sonnai visits the bazaar because she wants to buy some goods.*

Pupils perform the above task on their own.

Consider how to add extra detail to these sentences, using the compass directions.

**Geography afternoon**

Make a chart listing the jobs the pupils do at home and the jobs Sonnai does. Discuss the similarities and differences.



## **Day five** text level 21

**Resources**

Day four's sentences; line drawings; activity sheet 1; activity sheet 2; activity sheet 6 (Explanation layout)

Read a pupil's example of day four's sentences (OHT). Consider the layout of explanation writing. Focus on titles, subtitles, paragraphs and illustrations.

Write one of yesterday's sentences on the board. Give it a subtitle and add detail to it using activity sheet 1 and activity sheet 2. Then create a paragraph in a formal writing style.

*Flowers in the fields*

*Afterwards Sonnai runs to the fields, in order to gather flowers and create garlands. A garland is a circle of flowers worn like a necklace on special occasions. The fields are 200 metres south of Sonnai's family's house.*

Pupils write a detailed explanation of Sonnai's mobility map for 30 minutes, using either IT or activity sheet 6. Include a title, subtitles, paragraphs and line drawings. Check spellings using the spell check or dictionaries and display with the mobility map.

**Geography afternoon**

Look at a variety of different maps and focus on scale and compass directions

## Week two

### **Day six** text level 17

**Resources**

Mobility map

Look at the mobility map. Use this as a framework to design mobility maps for the class. Draw an example on the board (including a scale and compass directions if possible).

Brainstorm places the pupils visit (nouns) and list them on the board. Write a present tense action verb next to each noun, eg *visit shops, rush to park*. Label the nouns and action verbs in the appropriate places on the mobility map. Add a symbol or a sketch to represent each place visited.

Pupils perform the task on their own.

Pupils present their mobility maps to the class, explaining what they show.

**Geography afternoon**

Consider the means of transport pupils use to travel to the places identified on their mobility maps and compare them with Sonnai's. Draw a map of the local area and label the roads, railway lines, train stations, bus stops, car parks, bicycle lanes, footpaths, open space, traffic congestion and areas of pollution. Then draw an ideal future map showing how you would like to improve the area.



### **Day seven** text level 15

**Resources**

Pupils' mobility maps

Look at a pupil's mobility map. Revise features of explanation writing.

Brainstorm titles for the mobility map, subtitles for each place and temporal connectives. Add these to the mobility map.

Pupils perform the task on their own.

Develop explanation sentences, using words on the mobility map.

### **Day eight** text levels 20 and 21

**Resources**

Pupils' mobility maps; activity sheet 6 (photocopy to A3)

Revise the layout of explanation writing. Focus on titles, subtitles, paragraphs and illustrations.

Develop sentences from the words on the mobility map in the formal writing style of day five.

Include temporal connectives, nouns, present tense action verbs, causal connectives and detail. Activity sheet 6 can be used to help structure pupils' writing.

*Travelling to school*

*First Simon walks to school with his mother in order to study his favourite subjects and meet his friends. Simon travels along four roads to reach his school and the journey takes 20 minutes.*

Pupils write an explanation of their mobility maps for 30 minutes, using either IT or activity sheet 6. Include a title, subtitles, paragraphs and sketches. Check spellings using the spell check or dictionaries and display.

## **Day nine** text level 19

**Resources**

Mobility map; pupils' mobility maps; pupils' explanations of Sonnai's mobility map; pupils' explanations of their mobility maps; activity sheet 7 (Questionnaire – photocopy to A3)

Look at the two mobility maps (OHT) and read the two explanations (OHT).

Complete the questionnaire as a class. This enables pupils to compare the two mobility maps.

Pupils perform the task on their own.

Pupils present their results. Focus on the last section, which considers pupils' opinions.

## **Day ten** text level 22

**Resources**

Pupils' questionnaires; activity sheet 8 (Prompt sheet – photocopy to A3)

Look at one of the questionnaires and activity sheet 8 (OHT).

Use the questionnaire and the prompt sheet to develop formal sentences comparing the two mobility maps.

Pupils write a comparison of the two mobility maps for 30 minutes, using IT. Include paragraphs, edit using the spell check and display.

# Mobility map

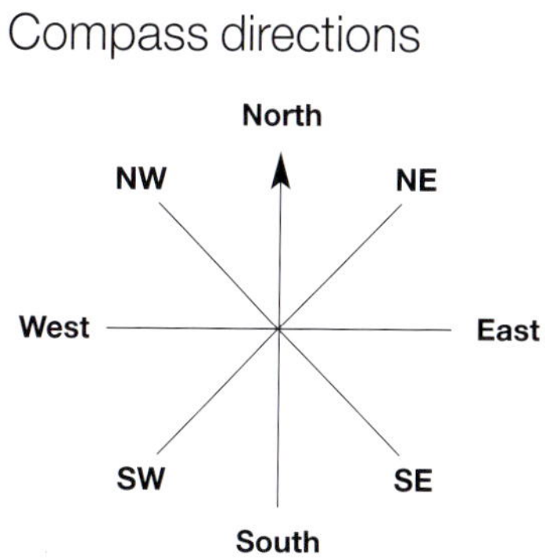

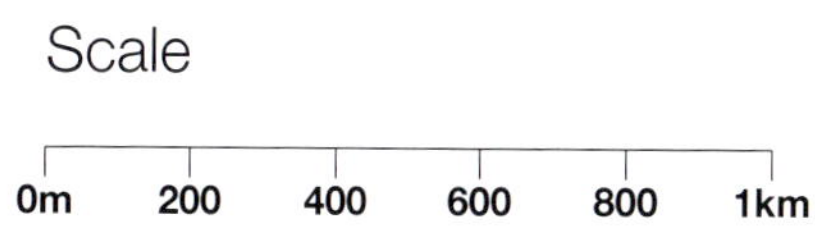




**tube well**

**pond**

**playground**

**bazaar**

**animal pens**

**friend's house**

**fields**

**cyclone shelter**

**school**

# Activity sheet 1 step 1 • Sonnai's recount

The map you can see is called a mobility map. It shows the places I visit on Kukri Mukri, the island where I live in Bangladesh. My house is in the middle of the map.

This morning I took scraps to the animal pens. I fed the ducks and chickens. Then I went to the tube well with my mother. We collected water.

After that, I walked to school. We learnt about numbers, food and what to do in a disaster. At break time I ran to the playground and played a game.

I walked to my friend's house after school and ate food. Next we went to the pond. We looked at the wildlife and caught insects. Then we picked beautiful flowers in the fields and made them into necklaces.

I went to the market at the weekend with my family. We bought some rice and other things. My father bought me a bracelet.

Two months ago I ran to the cyclone shelter with my family. The cyclone shelter protected us from the winds and flooding, so I was not scared.

# Activity sheet 1 step 2 • Sonnai's recount

The map you can see is called a mobility map. It shows the places I visit on Kukri Mukri, the island where I live in Bangladesh. My house is in the middle of the map.

Early this morning I carried two buckets of scraps to the animal pens. I fed the ducks and chickens. Then I walked to the tube well with my mother. We collected water in big pots.

After that, I walked to school. At school we learnt about maths, Bengali (which is our language), food, and what to do in a disaster. At break time I ran to the playground and played *dolna chhut* with my friends. *Dolna chhut* is a game played by girls in Bangladesh.

I wandered to my friend's house after school and ate some food. Next we went to the pond. We watched the wildlife and caught insects. Then we picked beautiful flowers in the fields and made them into garlands.

I went to the market at the weekend with my family. We bought rice, salt and oil to cook with. My father bought me a bracelet.

Two months ago there was a cyclone and I hurried to the cyclone shelter with my family. The cyclone shelter is very tall and made of concrete. It protected us from the winds and flooding, so I was not scared.

# Activity sheet 1 step 3 • Sonnai's recount

The map you can see is called a mobility map. It shows the places I often visit on Kukri Mukri, the small island where I live in Bangladesh. My house is in the centre of the map.

Early this morning I carried two buckets of scraps to the animal pens and fed the ducks and chickens. The pens are near my house. Then I walked to the tube well with my mother. We collected water in big pots and the whole journey took half an hour.

After that, I travelled to school on foot. At school we learnt about our language, Bengali. We also learnt about mathematics, food and disaster preparedness. Break was the best time of the day. I raced to the playground and played *dolna chhut* with my friends. *Dolna chhut* is a game played by girls in Bangladesh.

I wandered to my friend's house after school and ate some food. Next we visited the pond. We observed the wildlife and caught insects. Then we picked beautiful flowers in the fields near my house and prepared garlands.

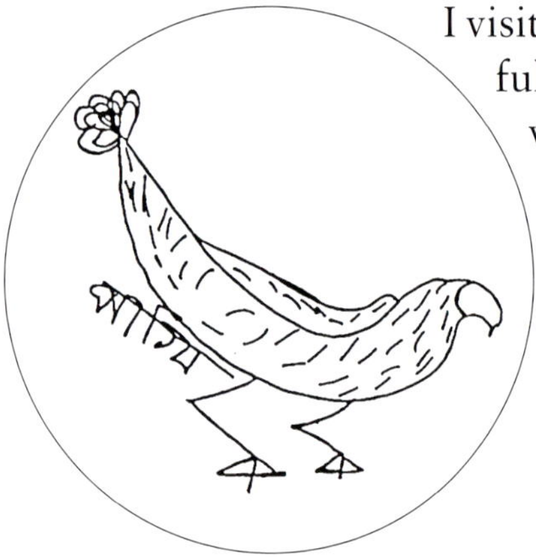

I visited the bazaar at the weekend with my family. It was full of people and we bought rice, salt and kerosene which were really heavy. My father bought me a bangle.

Two months ago there was a cyclone warning. I hurried to the shelter. It's over 10 metres high and made of concrete. It protected us from the winds and flooding. It wasn't a strong cyclone, so I wasn't too scared.

# Activity sheet 1 step 4 • Sonnai's recount

The mobility map highlights the places I regularly visit on Kukri Mukri, the small island where I live in the Bay of Bengal, Bangladesh. My house is situated in the centre of the map.

Soon after daybreak this morning I lugged two buckets of scraps to the animal pens and fed the ducks and chickens. The pens are to the north-west of my house. Then I walked to the tube well with my mother. We collected water in enormous pots and the entire journey took half an hour. My family washed, drank, cooked and cleaned with this water.

Soon after, I travelled almost a kilometre to school on foot. This took me 20 minutes. At school I learnt many subjects, including mathematics, Bengali, nutrition and disaster preparedness. However, break was my favourite time of day, because I raced to the playground and played *dolna chhut* with my friends. This is a popular girl's game in Bangladesh.

I strolled to my friend's house after school where I enjoyed some food. Next we visited the pond. We observed the wildlife and captured insects. Then we picked beautiful flowers in the fields south of my house and prepared garlands for special occasions.

I visited the bazaar at the weekend with my family. It's more than one kilometre from our house, and always full of people. We bought rice, salt and kerosene, which were really heavy to carry home. My father also bought me a bangle for being helpful.

Two months ago there was a cyclone warning. I hurried to the shelter. It's over 10 metres high and made of concrete. It protected us from the winds and flooding. It wasn't a severe cyclone, so I wasn't too scared.

# Activity sheet 2 • Mobility map outline

Title ____________________

Subtitle

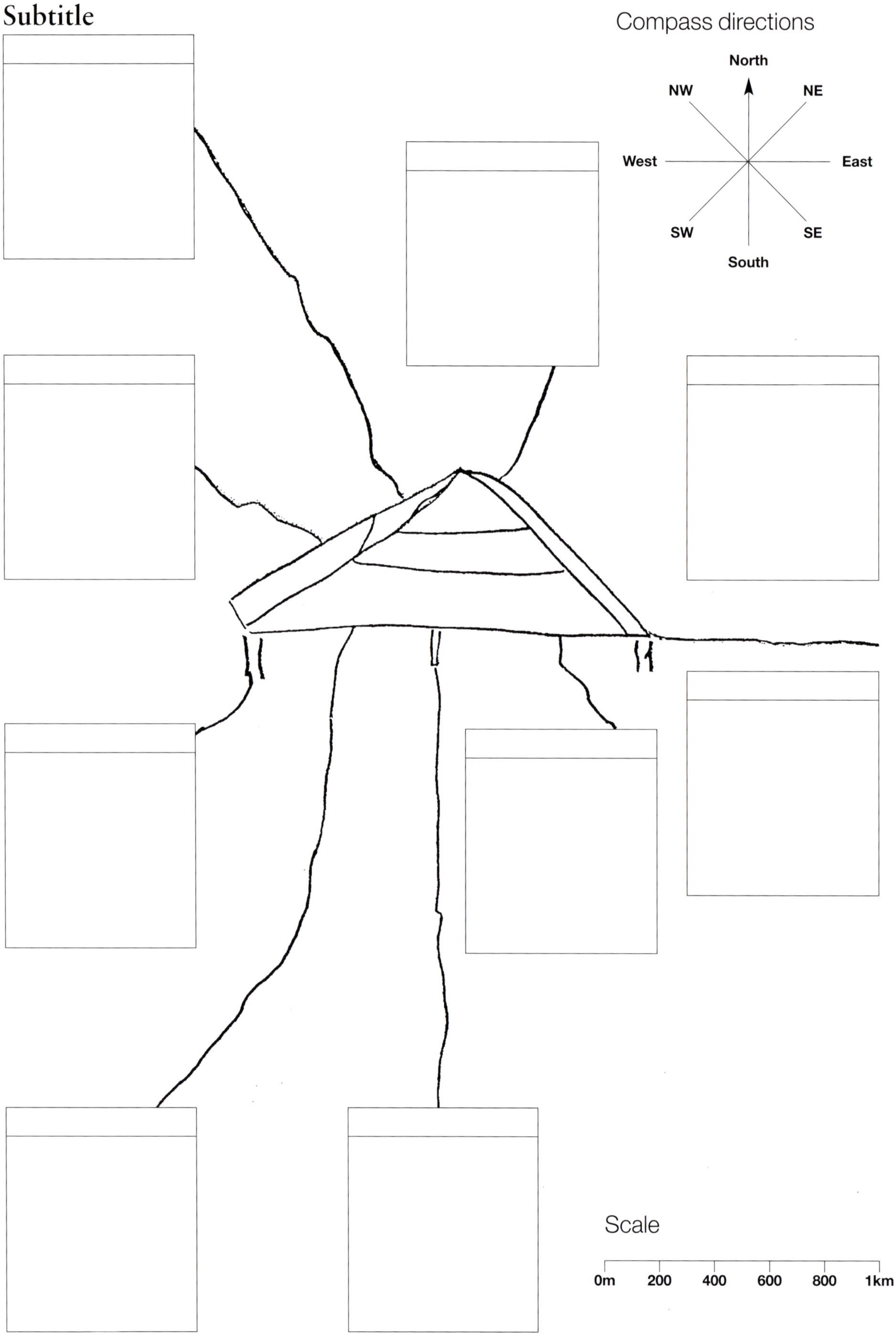

# Activity sheet 3 • Action verb word bank

| | | |
|---|---|---|
| **feed**  | **hurry** | **visit**  |
| **haul** | **protect** | **travel** |
| **proceed** | **enjoy**  | **study**  |
| **choose** | **pick**  | **trap** |
| **walk**  | **defend** | **journey** 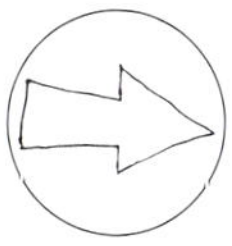 |
| **attend** | **capture** | **collect** |
| **play**  | **observe** 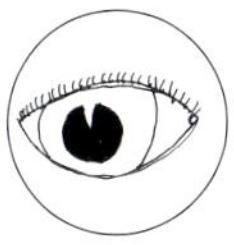 | **view** |
| **gather** | **run** | **amble** |
| **eat**  | **prepare** | **race** |
| **stroll** |  **learn** | **sprint** |
| **lug** | **buy**  | **obtain** |
| **create** | **rush** | **dart** |

# Activity sheet 4 • Words to do with time

**Later**

**Periodically**

**Every day**

**Next**

**Finally**

**Occasionally**

**At break time**

**Every afternoon**

**Following**

**Sometimes**

**Early in the morning**

**Then**

**First**

**Afterwards**

**Secondly**

**From time to time**

**Subsequently**

**In emergencies**

# Activity sheet 5 • Building sentences

Sonnai ________ to her friend's house

Sonnai ________ to the fields

Sonnai ________ to the tube well

Sonnai ________ to the playground

Sonnai ________ the bazaar

Sonnai ________ to the cyclone shelter

Sonnai ________ the pond

Sonnai ________ to school

Sonnai ________ two buckets of scraps to the animal pens

because she wants to

as a means to

in order to

as a way of

________ flowers and ________ garlands

________ the ducks and chickens

________ food

________ interesting subjects

________ herself from the winds and flooding

________ water

________ wildlife and ________ insects

________ some goods

________ *dolna chhut* with her friends

## Activity sheet 6

Title ______________________________

Subtitle ____________________

Drawing

Subtitle ____________________

Drawing

Subtitle ____________________

Drawing

Subtitle ____________________

Drawing

## Line drawings

pond

animal pens

friend's house

playground

tube well

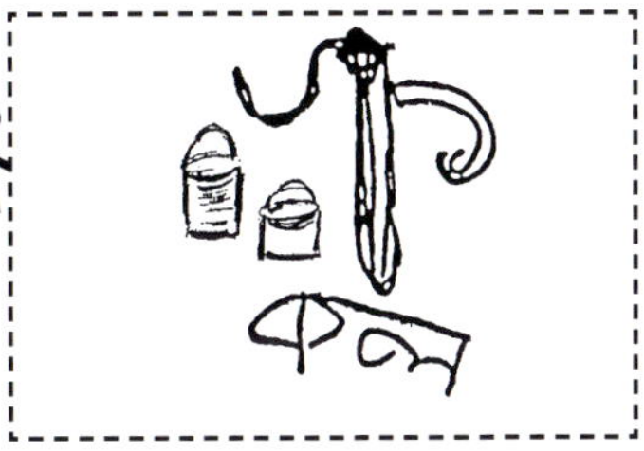


school

cyclone shelter

bazaar

fields

pond

animal pens

friend's house

playground

tube well

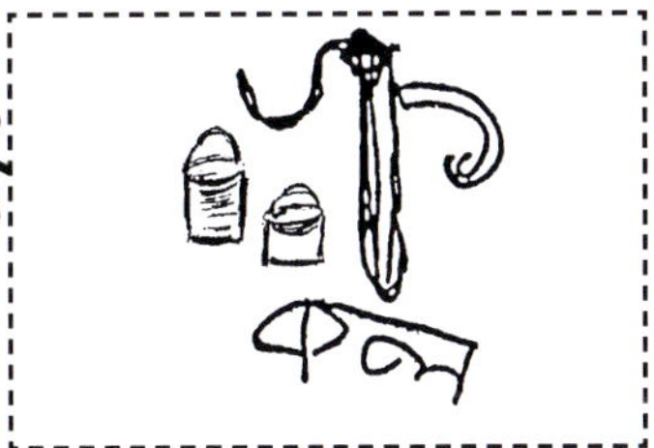


school

cyclone shelter

bazaar

fields

# Activity sheet 7 • Questionnaire

Look at the list of places Sonnai visits. Tick the boxes below if you go there too.

- ☐ Animal pens
- ☐ Tube well
- ☐ School
- ☐ Playground
- ☐ Friend's house
- ☐ Pond
- ☐ Fields/Park
- ☐ Bazaar/Shops
- ☐ Cyclone shelter

List three of the places both you and Sonnai visit and answer the questions.

| Place | What does Sonnai do here? | What do you do here? |
|---|---|---|
| | | |
| | | |
| | | |

Which of the places you visit would you like to show Sonnai and why?

________________________________________

________________________________________

________________________________________

Which of the places Sonnai visits would you like to see and why?

________________________________________

________________________________________

________________________________________

## Activity sheet 8 • Prompt sheet

Use the questionnaire and this prompt sheet to help you to write a comparison between Sonnai's mobility map and your mobility map.

Title

A comparison between ____________________ and ____________________

| Sentence starters | Linking words | Endings |
|---|---|---|
| Sonnai visits | However | Finally |
| Simon visits | Compared to | In conclusion |
| They are similar because | Whereas | We can see |
| They both | But | Having looked at |
| They are different because | Although | Simon feels |
| They contrast because | While | The final point is |



Examples

**Sonnai** visits the tube well, **whereas** *Simon* has running water in his house.

**They both** attend school, **but** Sonnai studies Bengali and *Simon* studies English.

**In conclusion**, *Simon* has a very different life to Sonnai. **However**, he would like to visit Bangladesh one day to explain his mobility map to Sonnai.

# Further information

## Examples of Reflect graphics

**The following Reflect graphics can be used within the literacy hour.**

## A farming calendar

This calendar shows farming workloads and how they affect people's lives in an area. People in Reflect circles discuss the following questions:

- Which is the best time of the farming year and why?
- Which is the most stressful time of year and why?
- Can you think of action points to make certain times of year less stressful?

## A farming map

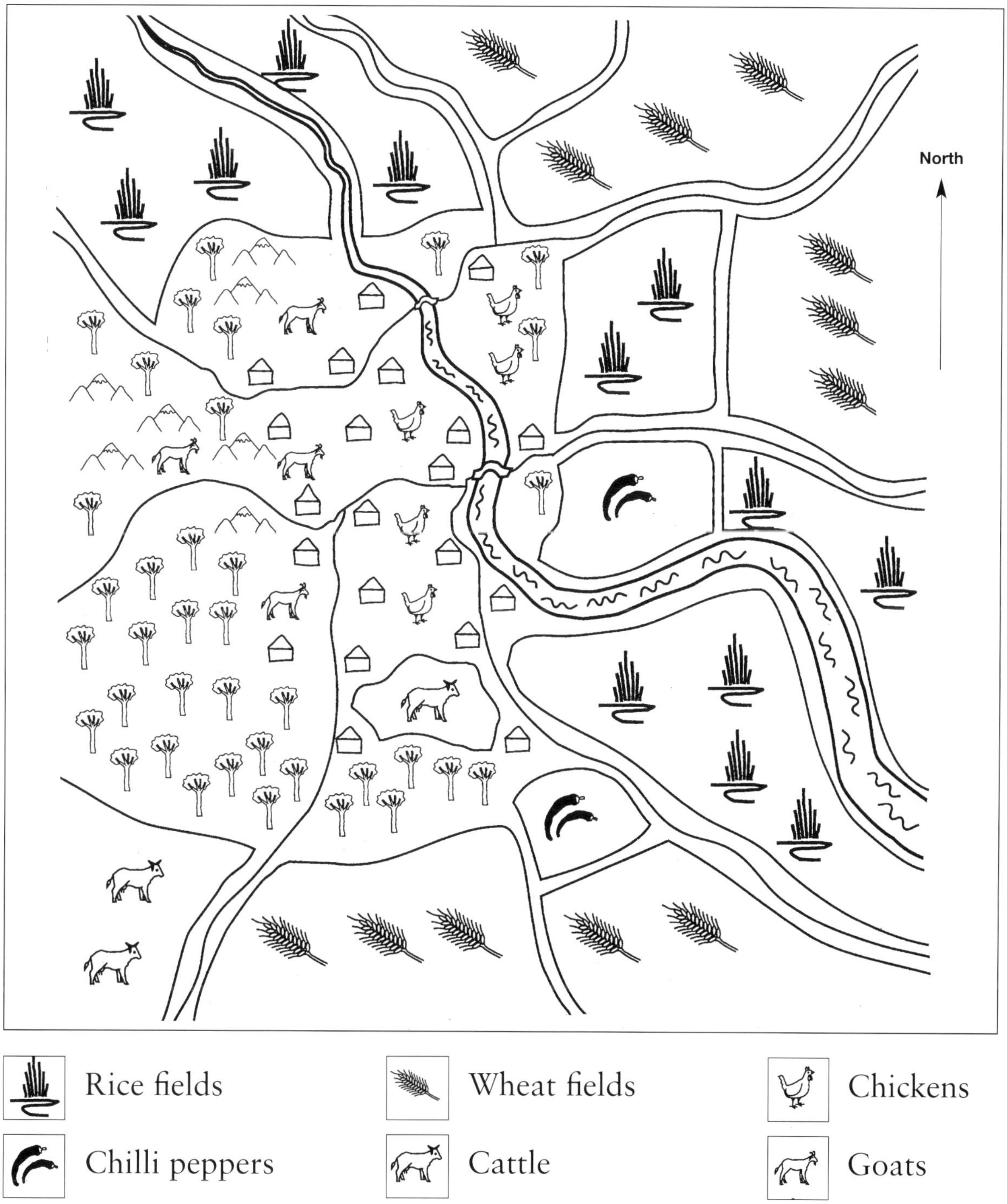


The map shows how land is used in an area. People in Reflect circles discuss the following questions:

- How many types of animals are there?
- What are these animals used for?
- What crop grows well near the river?
- What crop grows well away from the river?
- Can you think of action points to improve farming methods in the area?

## A transect walk

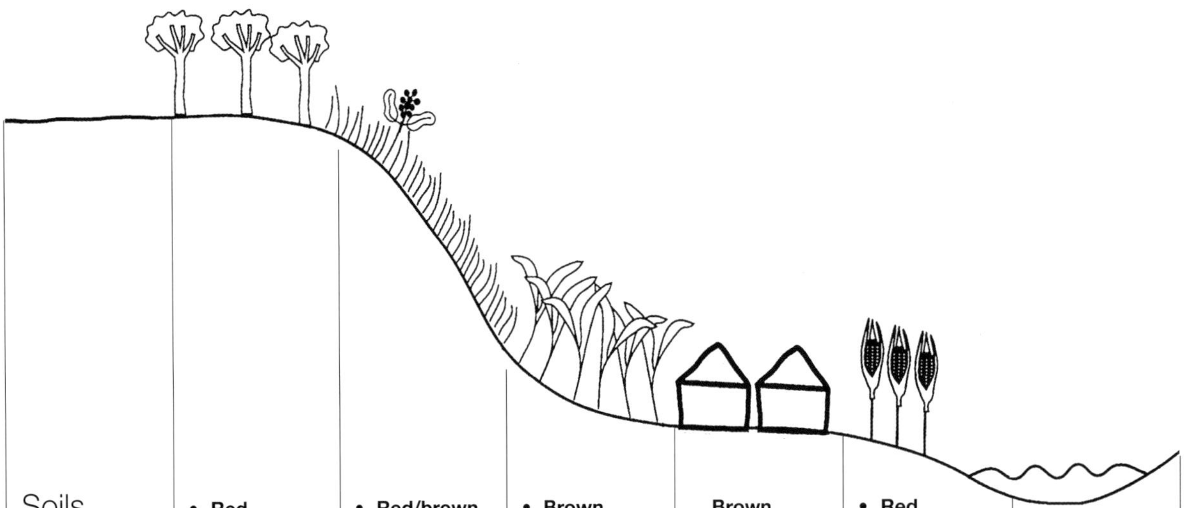

| | | | | | | |
|---|---|---|---|---|---|---|
| Soils | • Red | • Red/brown | • Brown | Brown | • Red | |
| Crops | • Fruit trees | • Coffee<br>• Grass land | • Bananas<br>• Maize<br>• Beans<br>• Peppers | • Vegetables | • Maize<br>• Beans<br>• Peppers | |
| Problems | • Foxes | • Too many weeds | • Flooding | • Flooding<br>• Not many people can read or write | • Flooding | |
| Solutions | • Put a fence around the trees | • Grow more coffee<br>• Volunteers pull up the weeds | • Make the river banks stronger | • Make the river banks stronger<br>• Reflect programme | • Make the river banks stronger | |

The transect walk shows a path through a village. In Reflect circles information about the soils and crops is written down first. Then problems and solutions to the problems are added and discussed.

Why not make a transect walk for your local area and compare it with the one above?

## Timeline of a village

| | |
|---|---|
| 1970 | Fire destroyed the woodland |
| 1971 | A mosque was built in the village |
| 1979 | A centre for training carpenters started in the village |
| 1983 | Farmers started growing coffee |
| 1987 | A primary school was built in the village |
| 1990 | A new road was built leading to the village market |
| 1998 | Flooding destroyed 11 houses and the health centre |
| 2000 | The health centre was rebuilt |



The timeline shows major events in a village over 30 years. People in Reflect circles discuss the following questions:

- What major events might happen in the next 10 years?
- What major events would you like to happen in the next 10 years?
- Which of the events on the timeline were uncontrollable?
- Which of the following action points are the best:
  – tape older people talking about the events;
  – plan a day to remember a major event;
  – make a sign to mark where a major event happened?

## A money tree

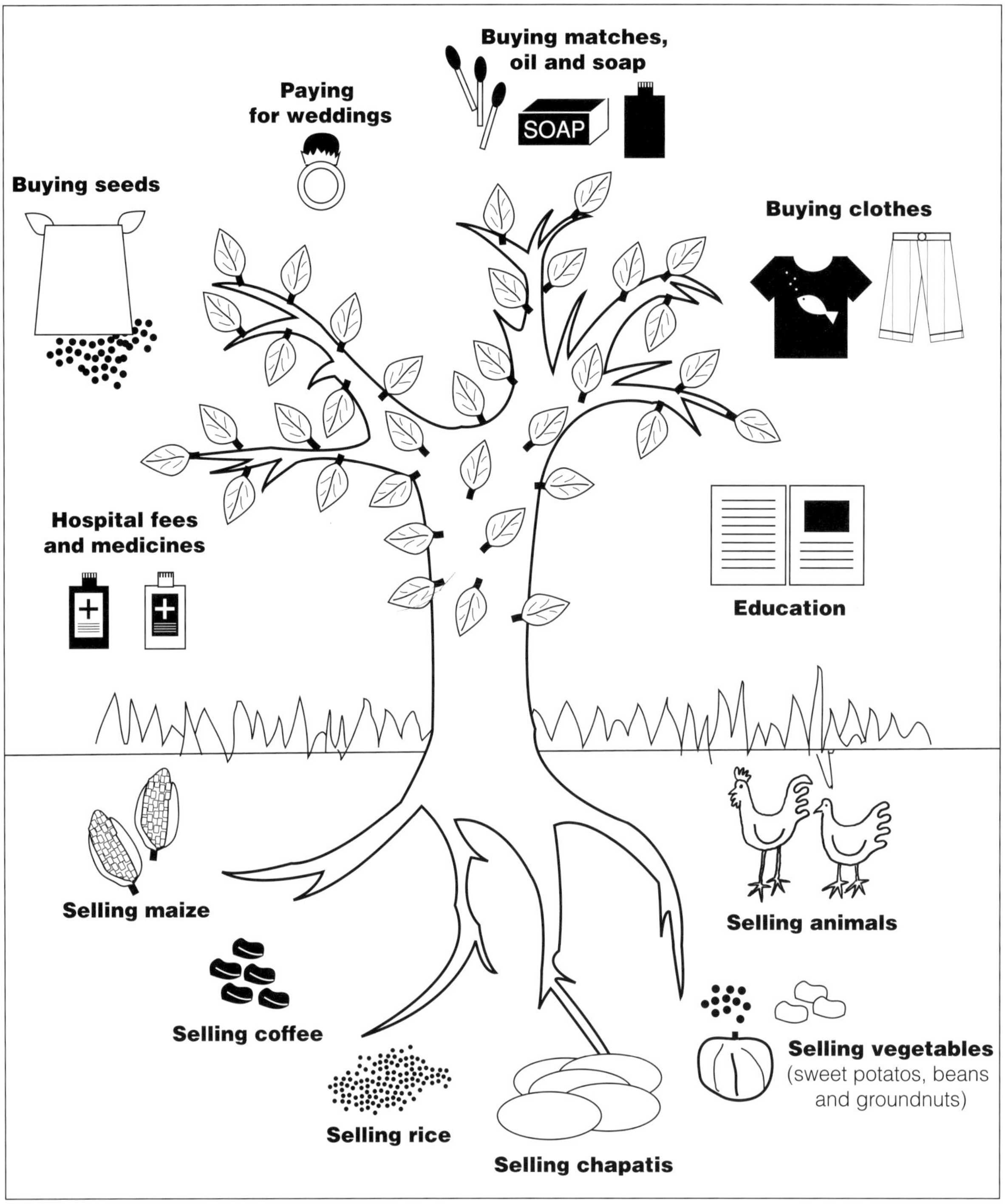


The roots of the tree show how people in an area make money and the branches show how they spend money. People in Reflect circles discuss the following questions:

- Do we spend more money than we make?
- Will the tree fall over if we spend more money than we make?
- Do we need to think of action points to improve the situation?

## A money calendar

| Month | J | F | M | A | M | J | J | A | S | O | N | D |
|---|---|---|---|---|---|---|---|---|---|---|---|---|
| How people make money | | | | | | | | | | | | |
| **Selling coffee** | | | | | | | | | | | | |
| **Selling rice** | | | | | | | | | | | | |
| **Selling vegetables** | | | | | | | | | | | | |
| **Selling maize** | | | | | | | | | | | | |
| **Selling animals** | | | | | | | | | | | | |
| **Selling chapatis** | | | | | | | | | | | | |
| How people spend money | | | | | | | | | | | | |
| **Hospital fees and medicines** | | | | | | | | | | | | |
| **Buying seeds** | | | | | | | | | | | | |
| **Paying for weddings** | | | | | | | | | | | | |
| **Buying clothes** | | | | | | | | | | | | |
| **Buying matches, oil and soap** | | | | | | | | | | | | |
| **Education** | | | | | | | | | | | | |

The calendar shows when people in an area make money and when they spend money. It also shows roughly how much they earn and spend. People in Reflect circles discuss the following questions:

- What is the best way of making money?
- What is the worst way of making money?
- What do people spend most money on?
- What do people spend least money on?
- What happens if some animals die?
- What happens if a child falls ill and needs to go to hospital?
- Can you think of action points to improve the situation?

## A workload calendar – men

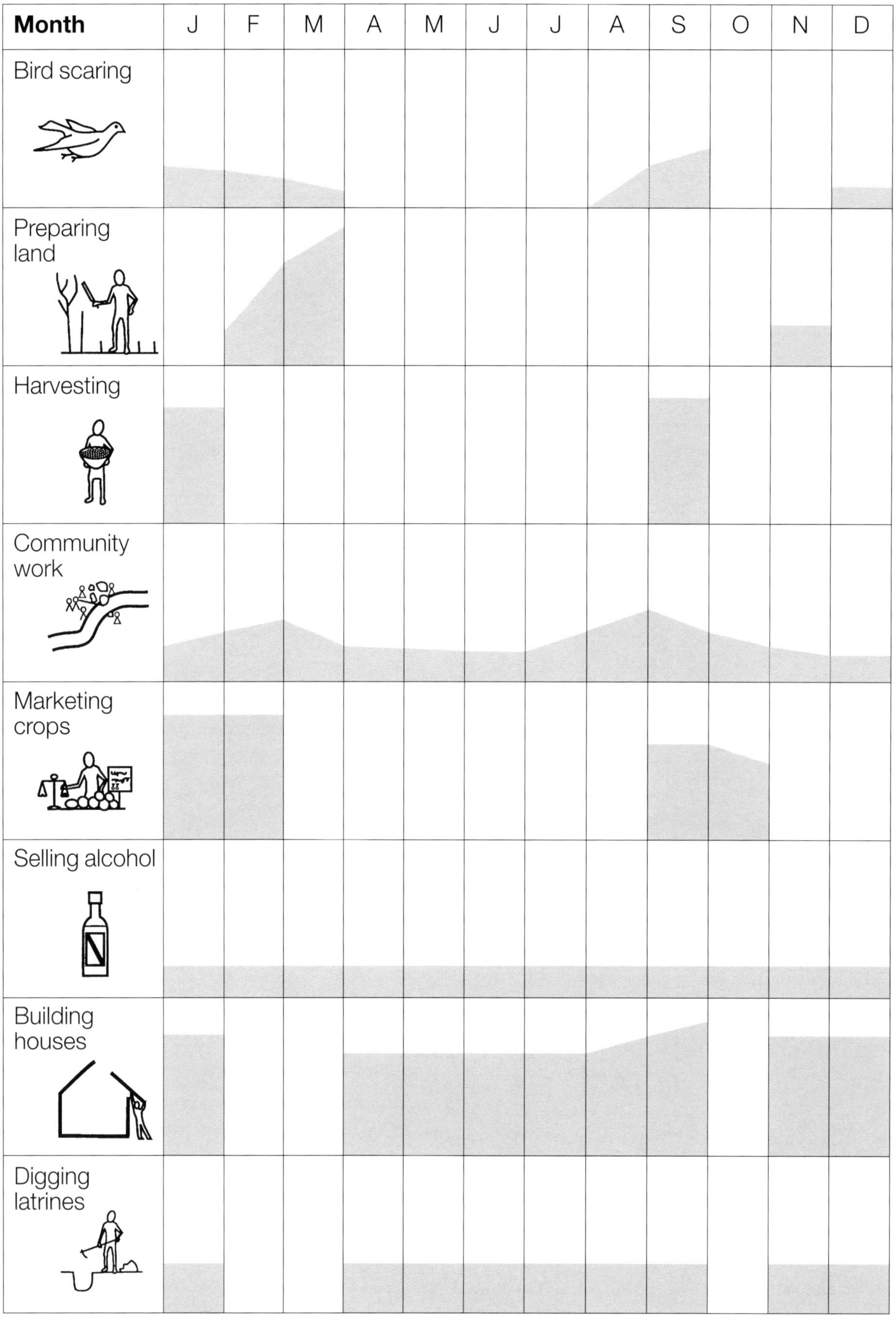


This calendar shows men's workload in an area.

## A workload calendar – women

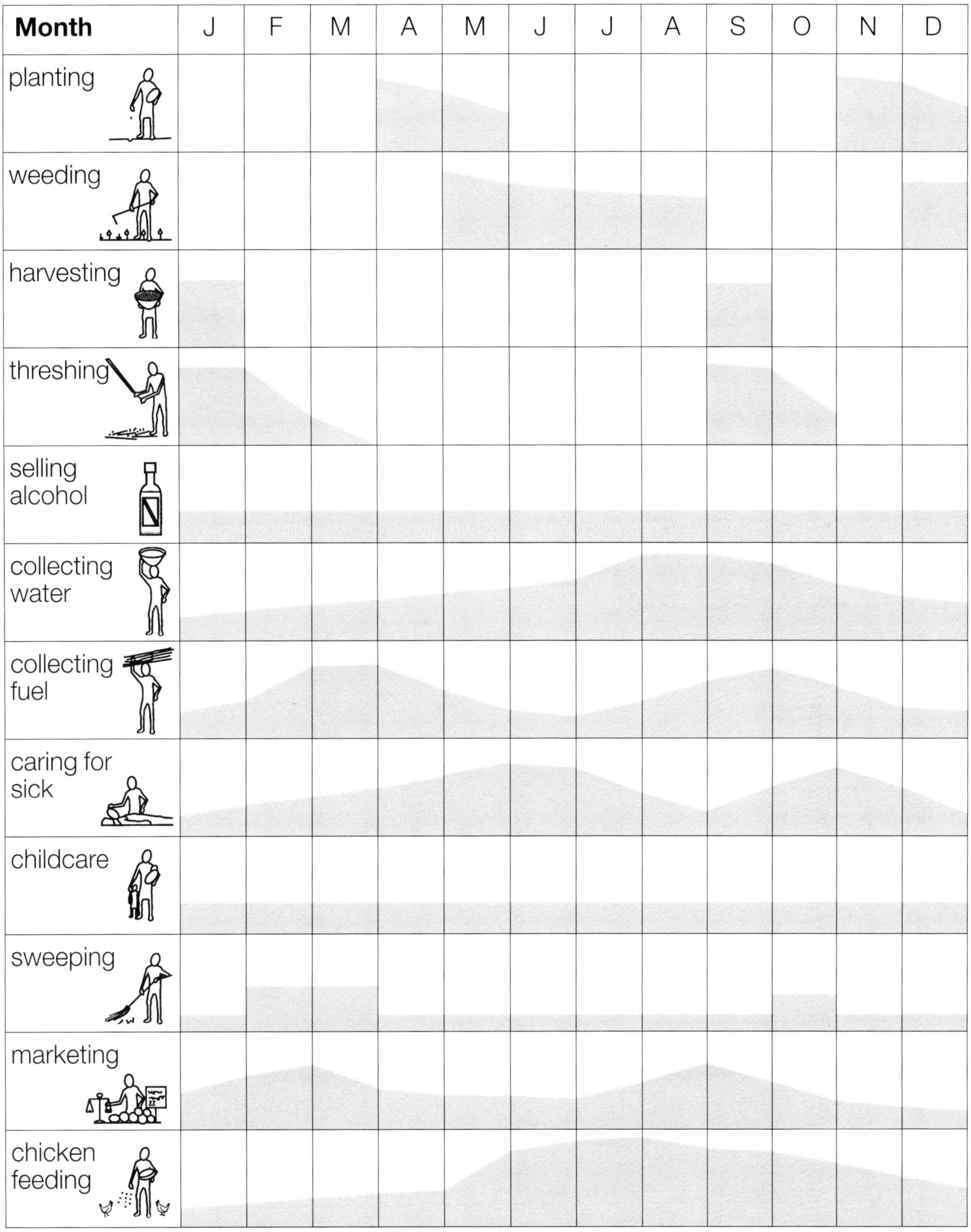




In Reflect circles the women's workload calendar is compared to the men's workload calendar. The people:

- look at the workloads of men and women in an area;
- decide whether the division of work is fair (eg Is cleaning work?);
- think of action points to improve the situation (eg swap workloads for a day).

## A travelling map

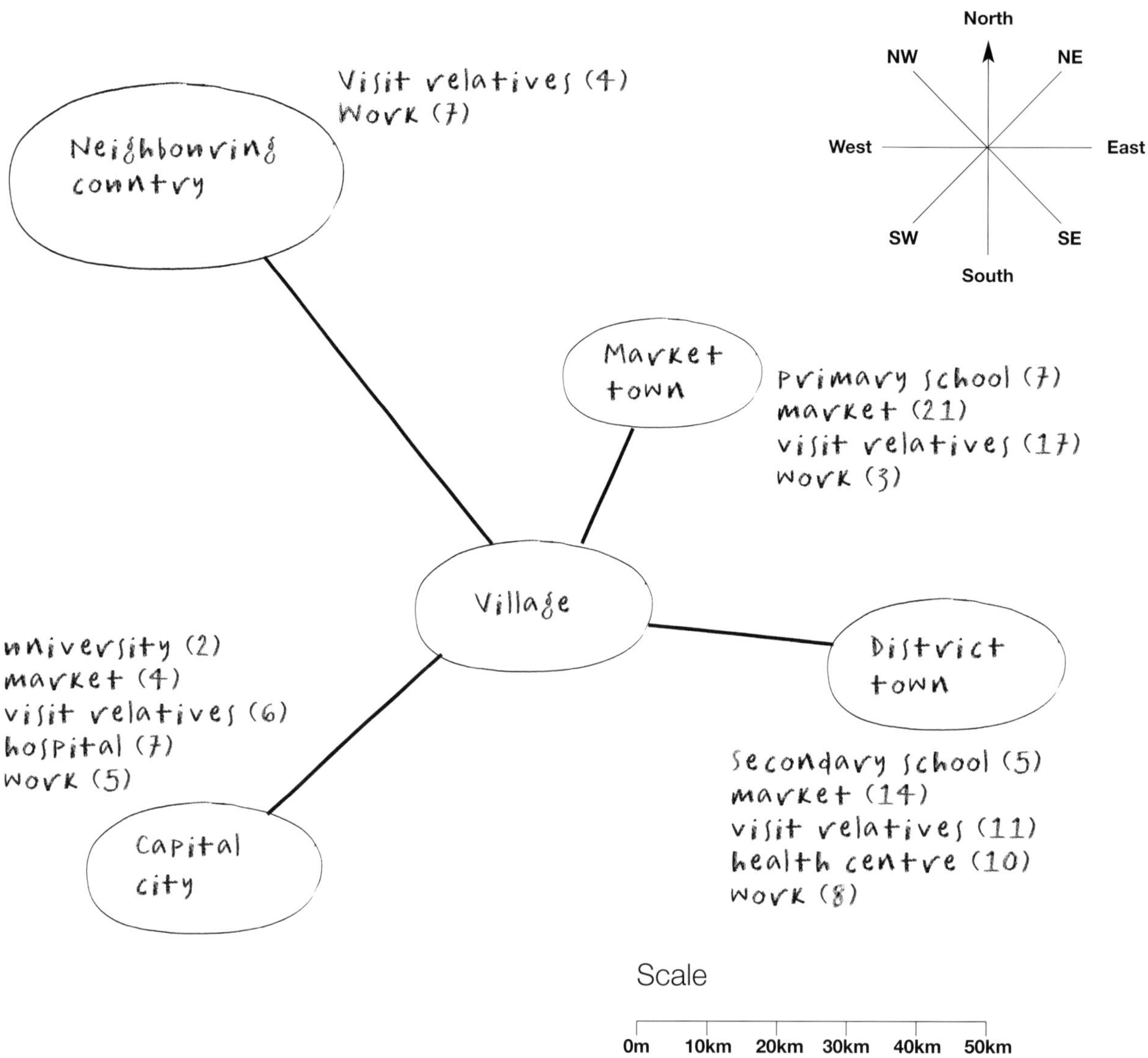


The map shows where people from a village travel to in one week. People in Reflect circles discuss the following questions:

- How many people live in the village?
- How many children and young people go to the primary school, secondary school and the university?
- Where is the primary school, secondary school and university?
- What are the problems facing people wanting to go to secondary school or university?
- Where is the nearest health centre and hospital?
- What are the problems for people who are ill?
- Where is the nearest market?
- What are the advantages of taking goods to a market near by?
- Can you think of any action points to improve the situation?

## A skills map

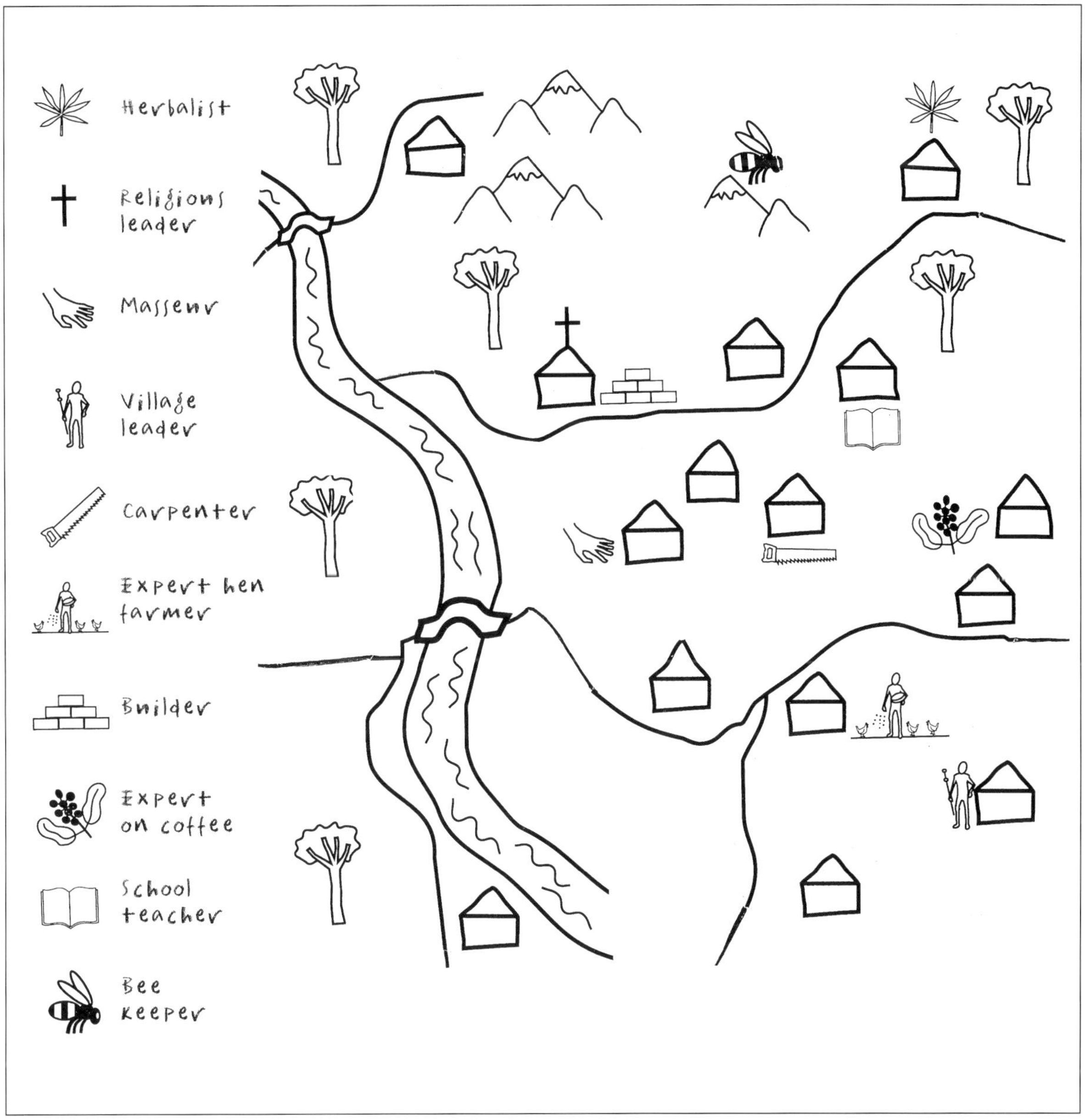


This map shows the special skills local people have. People in Reflect circles discuss the following questions:

- How many different skills do people have in the community?
- What skills do the people use every day?
- What skills do the people use occasionally?
- How did the people get their skills and how will they pass them on to others?
- Can you think of any action points to help pass the skills to other people?

# A map of the world

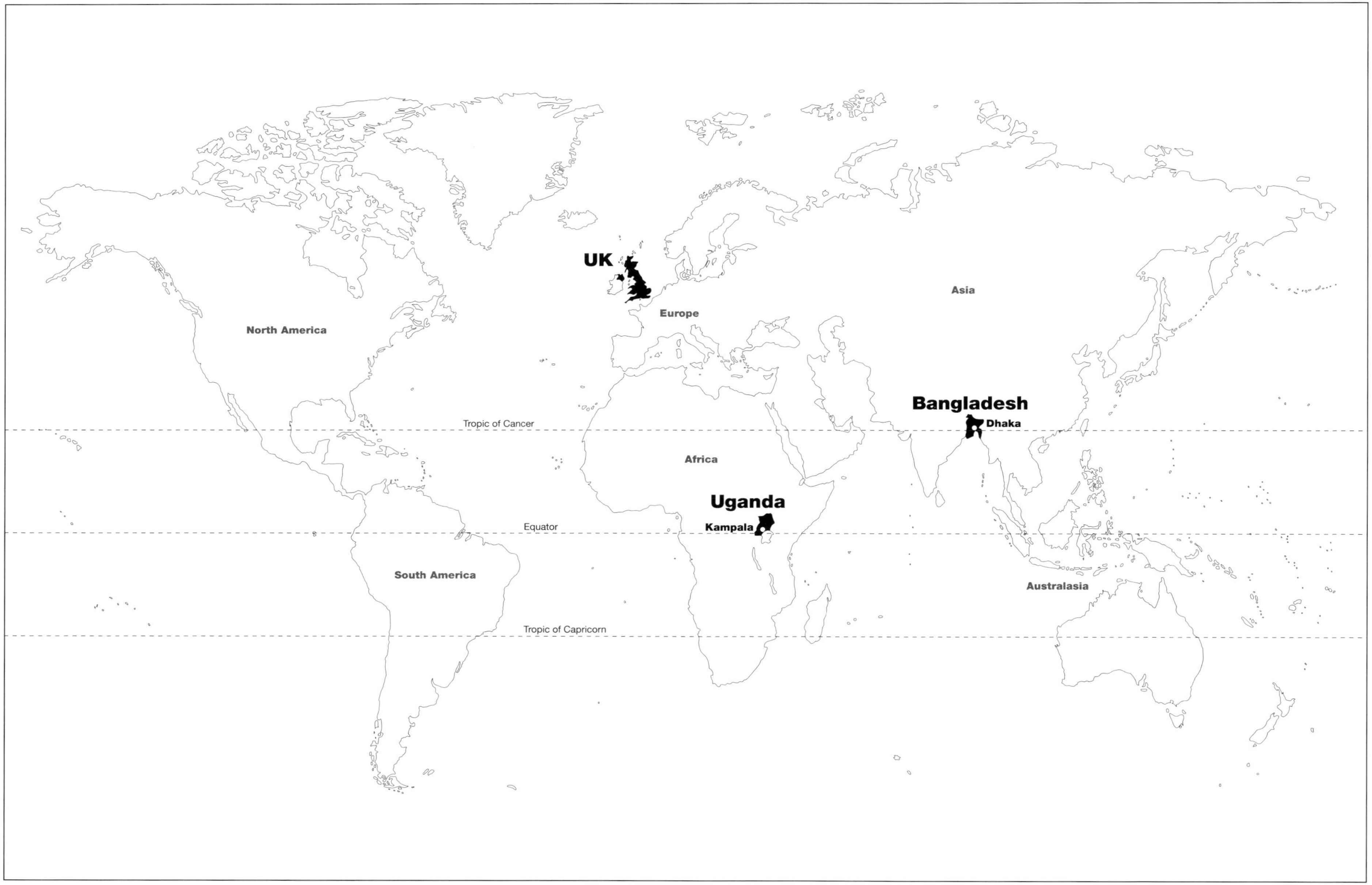

## A map of Uganda

**A map of Bangladesh**

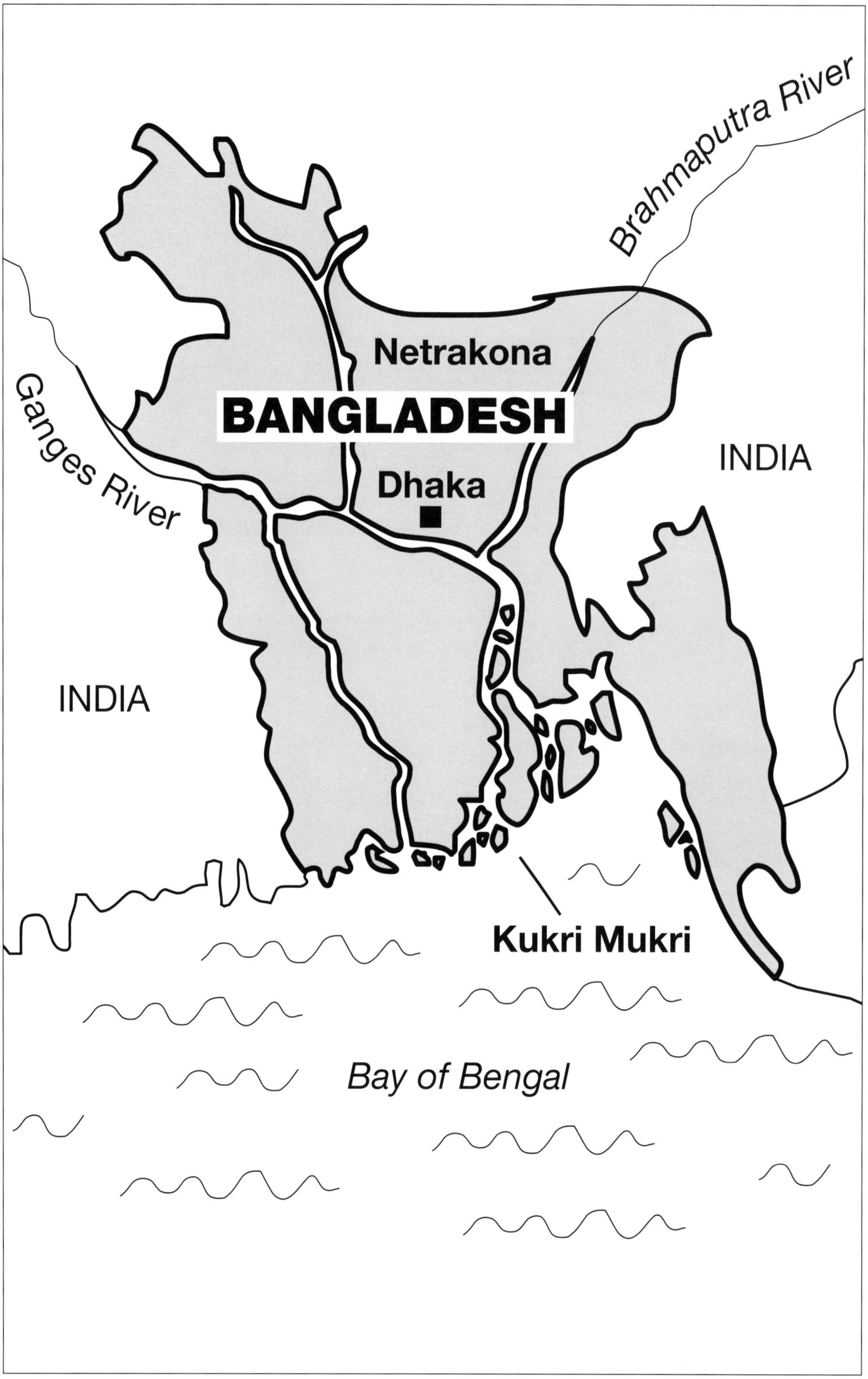

## Useful contacts

**Council for Education in World Citizenship**
15 St Swithin's Lane,
London EC4N 8AL
Telephone: 020 7929 5091
Website:www.cewc.org.uk

**Fair Trade Foundation**
Suite 204, 16 Baldwins Gardens,
London EC1N 7RJ
Telephone: 020 7405 5942
Website: www.fairtrade.org.uk

**Environmental Investigation Agency**
69 Old Street,
London EC1V 9HX
Telephone: 020 7490 7040
Website: www.eia-international.org.uk

**Kidscape** (information on bullying)
2 Grosvenor Gardens,
London SW1W 0DH
Telephone: 020 7730 3300
Website: www.kidscape.org.uk

**School Councils UK**
57 Etchingham Park Road, Finchley, London N3 2EB
Telephone: 020 8349 2459
Website: www.schoolcouncils.org.uk

**Transport 2000**
12–18 Hoxton Street,
London N1 6NG
Telephone: 020 7613 0743

**Women's Football Association**
9 Wyllyotts Place, Potters Bar, Hertfordshire EN6 2JD
Telephone: 01707 651 840
Website: www.the-fa.org.uk

## Other ActionAid resources for the literacy hour

*Footprints in the forest: a Chembakolli story*
A fiction big book for KS2 set in southern India.
Big book £17.25 / Individual reader £5.75

*Footprints* clipart CD
CD-ROM (Windows/Mac OS/RISC OS) £13.80

*From Beans to Batteries*
A fiction book set in the Peruvian village of Pampagrande.
Book £4.60

*Hadithi Nzuri* (a good story):
A review guide to children's literature from Africa, Asia and Latin America.
Book £6.90

*In the eye of the storm: life on an island in Bangladesh*
A non-fiction big book for KS2 set on the cyclone-prone island of Kukri Mukri.
Big book £17.25

*Mary, Juma and Simba the dog*
A fiction big book for KS2 set in Mombasa, Kenya.
Big book £17.25 / Individual reader £5.75

*Read all about it: Get your non-fiction texts on Kenya here!*
An interactive CD-ROM set in Mombasa, Kenya.
CD-ROM (Windows/Mac OS) £17.25

*Salamatu and Kandoni go missing*
A picture book set in the Ghanaian village of Nansoni.
Book £4.60

*Education for global citizenship – primary briefing*
A briefing paper indicating how ActionAid's resources can be used to bring a global dimension to the PSHE and citizenship curriculum.
Free

**For a catalogue contact:**
ActionAid Education,
Chataway House,
Leach Road,
Chard,
Somerset TA20 1FR
Telephone: 01460 23 8000
Facsimile: 01460 67 191
Email: deved@actionaid.org.uk
Website: www.actionaid.org/deved/

19
ACTIONAID

ঘূর্নি ঝড় আশ্রয় কেন্দ্র
কুকরী মুকরী সরকারী প্রাথমিক বিদ্যালয়
স্থাপিত ঃ- ১৯৪০ ইং
নতুন ভবন নির্মান ১৯৯৭/৯৮ ইং.

1
ACTIONAID

ACTIONAID

3
ACTIONAID

4

5
ACTIONAID

6 ACTIONAID

7 ACTIONAID

bisingo
bundimulangya
Kinga: 2
MAPU yebhyetungha byo muntu weka
endagililo
mucele
mbaa
koko
mbuli
Kitoke
mwani
nkoko
bugude
Kagisa
sabalo
nkwi

9
ACTIONAID

10
ACTIONAID

11
ACTIONAID

13
ACTIONAID

ACTIONAID

17
ACTIONAID

18
ACTIONAID